A Tapestry of Voices Approaching
John-Baptist de La Salle

Hernán Santos, FSC

Dedication:

To all who are beginning to know and follow the adventures of Saint John-Baptist de La Salle, who deeply believed in and was led by God's Providence.

Thanks:

To Brother Santiago Rodríguez Mancini and Brother Bruno Alpago, who always encouraged me and suggested corrections. To Brother William Mann, who helped with the foreword and editing for the English version.

To all the communities where I served over the years. You have been my source of joy and commitment.

Index

Foreword

When I first read the manuscript that you are now holding in your hands, a passage in an address that the late Brother Michel Sauvage prepared for delivery at the 41st General Chapter of 1986 came to mind:

> Through this decisive option of separation and of commitment [giving up his canonry in order to share his whole existence with the schoolmasters], a creative power can be seen in the person of John-Baptist de La Salle, leading him to fulfill a prophetic passage: "Behold, I shall make all things new" (Rev 21:5). De La Salle leaves an old, immobile Church to accede to a new one, or at least having freely consented to the creative force acting in and beyond him, he allows himself to be re-born to a new way of living the Church.

Brother Hernán Santos has gifted us, his readers, with a well-researched and deceptively simple re-telling of the story of a man many of us have come to know and admire. The tale Brother Hernán tells, one reflecting the joys and the anguish of a life well-lived in service of helping young people realize their dignity as the children of God, is as lyrical as it is profound; and his decision to have the story told in the first-person voice by a cast of characters who knew De La Salle intimately was brilliant.

These voices, which are woven together into a quite charming tapestry, invite contemplation of the passage of God in the life of a real human being who, like many of us, had both friends and enemies and who enjoyed a certain amount of success and a fair dose of self-doubt.

This journey of John-Baptist de La Salle, and his first Brother teachers, is itself the confirmation of the Founder's own advice to his 17th-century associates: "Providence performs miracles daily, and they cease only for those who have no trust."

The story of "bringing to birth in the Church a new kind of religious family of laymen, rooted in the Gospel, both in its external ministry and in its internal life" continues to attract and fire the imagination of countless educators, church ministers, and childcare workers today; and its re-telling is so very timely as Lasallians around the world commemorate the tercentenary of the once fragile Community of De La Salle's civil recognition by Letters Patent (September 28, 1724) and ecclesial approval by the Bull of Approbation (January 26, 1725).

And so I encourage you on the occasion of this anniversary – regardless of whether this is your first introduction to John-Baptist de La Salle or you are someone already well versed in the story of the Lasallian origins – to enjoy the time you're about to spend with the Founder's family, partners in mission, and admirers. Perhaps, like our author, you might even be heartened to recall – and perhaps even share – your own providential encounter with "La Salle."

Brother William Mann, FSC

Presentation

The 300th anniversary of the death of Saint John-Baptist de La Salle in 2019 served as an excuse for writing a series of stories published, between 2017 and 2019, in the magazine Asociados of the Lasallian District of Argentina-Paraguay. I was invited to undertake this adventure by Brother Santiago Rodríguez Mancini. I must confess that the challenge of writing these texts meaningfully allowed me to rediscover the figure of an exciting man whose life continues to inspire me profoundly.

I believe that all of us have approached De La Salle's work in different ways. Whatever corner of the world we are in, we have experienced a way of being disciples of Jesus, engaging in an apostolate, or, as we Lasallians like to say, a ministry, for the educational service of the poor. That life experience, which in my case had its beginnings in the catechesis given by the Brothers in my neighborhood, later led me to become a catechist. That was the starting point of a journey that made me fall more and more in love with the Lasallian charism and mission.

The stories presented here do not pretend to be a biography but rather an approach to the figure of the Founder by means of a narrative that combines historical figures, contexts, subjectivities, life experiences, and an interpretation from the narrator's perspective.

Each chapter is based on research done on the life of the character presented.[1] It is an attempt to understand their life history, personality, emotions, thoughts ... and to look for references to time, place, culture and circumstance. All of this is to try to "get under the skin of the character" and, thus, to narrate, imaginatively reconstructing situations, scenarios, and dialogues, realizing how very different they are from how we live today.

The footnotes seek to help us better understand the historical aspects, characters, places, works, and situations that make up the French culture of the *Ancien Régime*. The same can be said of the images that accompany the texts, most of which were taken from the beautiful iconographic work of Brother Émile Rousset.[2] Others come from the wonderful world of the Internet.

I must clarify that the chapters were written at different times, places, and circumstances. They are, therefore, influenced by context. Most of the time, the writing took place in the early mornings in Capiíbary [Paraguay], before going to work. At other times, when circumstances permitted, I was able to go to Fernando de la Mora's house, where my vocational story began. Often, I was in the novitiate at Cordoba [Argentina], where I could have access to abundant and rich literature. The final chapters bear witness to the serene complicity of nature and the mate[3] at sunset in a square somewhere, or perhaps even in Dublin's Botanical Gardens.

The attempt to narrate interpretively from the perspective of the characters who were in contact with John-Baptist[4] de La

---

[1] At the end of each chapter, readers are provided with a listing of the texts consulted for the writing of the chapter (almost all were Spanish-language texts). However, an attempt has been made with this translation to provide, whenever possible, English-language translations of the resources consulted.

[2] Cf. *Cahiers lasalliens 49: L'iconographie de saint Jean-Baptist de La Salle* by Joseph-Aurélien Cornet FSC and Émile Rousset FSC (Rome: FSC, 1989).

[3] A traditional South American hot caffeine-infused herbal drink.

[4] As he was known to his French confreres, relatives, friends, and society.

Salle made it possible for me to approach the Founder from a more human point of view. In that attempt, the characters in the stories embodied traits of people I know and admire. This phenomenon did not just happen with the characters; something similar also occurred while writing, for I was influenced by authors as diverse as Mamerto Menapache, Augusto Roa Bastos, Bram Stoker, and Johanna Spyri.

However, the one who inspired the basic idea was the German biblical scholar, Gerd Theissen, with his book *The Shadow of the Galilean.*[5]

There is another intention to narrating in this way, i.e., to ensure a more pleasant experience for the reader seeking to get closer to the person of John-Baptist de La Salle. The invitation is that, through these perspectives, the reader will identify something within his or her own life experiences.

Of course, many more characters could still be found and addressed, and more significant insights could undoubtedly be brought to light. The invitation to the reader remains to continue from his or her own vital place within this narrative adventure.

---

[5] *The Shadow of the Galilean: The Quest of the Historical Jesus in Narrative Form* by Gerd Theissen and translated by John Bowden (Minneapolis, MN: Fortress Press, 2007).

Family Memories

Perrette Lespagnol Moët (1615 - 1691)

I still remember, as if it were yesterday, the hustle and bustle at the *Hôtel de La Cloche* where my daughter Nicole Moët de Brouillet and her husband Louis de La Salle lived. They had married and were now expecting their first child. The prevailing anxiety could be felt in the air: hurried steps, preparations everywhere. Everyone was eagerly awaiting the new member of the family. I was no exception. My first

Hôtel de La Cloche, where John-Baptist was born.

grandchild was about to be born, and his parents had already decided to name him John-Baptist.

It is hard to find words to describe that day, April 30th, 1651. Deeply engraved in my memory is the birth, the joy of the whole house, the happy faces of his parents, and the company of our closest relatives and friends. It seemed as if the whole city of Rheims was celebrating. That same day, the child was baptized, and my husband, Jean Moët, and I proudly and gladly assumed the role of John-Baptist's godparents. From then on, a deep affection would unite us.

I watched my grandson grow up. I witnessed the education he received at home until he was nine years old. Like a good godmother, I taught him the prayers and everything related to our faith. But, above all, he very much enjoyed it when I read the lives of the saints to him. I could see his interest, and his little eyes showed me his desire to be like them. There was no lack of occasions when he accompanied me to church to pray and contemplate the presence of God. He once mentioned to me that he wanted to be a priest...

Nicole Moët, mother of John-Baptist.

Over time, the family grew, siblings arrived, but four of them died in infancy. This was the case with Remy, Marie-Anne, Jean-Louis, and Simon. Infant mortality was a serious matter[6] in those days.

In addition to John-Baptist, the oldest, there survived two girls, Marie and Rose-Marie, and four boys, Jacques-Joseph, Jean-Louis, Pierre, and Jean-Rémy. As you can see, John-Baptist had ten siblings. Three of them, like their older brother, consecrated their lives to God. Rose-Marie entered the convent, and Jacques-Joseph and Jean-Louis became priests.

---

[6] According to Robert Darnton, based on other authors: "Life was a ruthless struggle against death everywhere at the dawn of modern France. In Crulai, Normandy, 263 out of every 1,000 babies died before their first birthday during the 17th century. This is in contrast to the 20 who die today. 45% of the French people born in the 18th century died before the age of ten. Few children reached adulthood before at least one of their parents had died. Very few mothers managed to live to the end of their childbearing years because death prevented them from doing so." Perrette had ten children, of whom only five reached the age of majority.

But let me continue to tell you about John-Baptist, whom I still see running around the family's vineyards.[7] At the age of ten, he had to go to school. In Rheims, the *Collège des Bons Enfants* had an excellent reputation. John-Baptist was always very responsible and serious. He liked his studies and worked hard to get good grades. But what few of us in the family imagined was the desire that he kept in his heart. He wanted to dedicate his life to God. He made this known to his parents, who already had some sense of it. Many in the family expected him to embrace the same profession as his father, who practiced law at the Court of Appeal in Rheims, dependent on the Parliament of Paris. But Louis and Nicole were people of faith and agreed to let John-Baptist receive the tonsure[8] in the archbishop's chapel at Rheims. Since then, my grandson has worn this mark indicating his vocational pursuit and intentions.

Everything related to faith and the Church attracted him: Masses, baptisms, prayers. ... so it was that, at a young age, he was godfather at the baptism of his brothers Jean-Louis and Pierre.[9] My grandson felt at ease in the church and liked the prayers and songs of the canons[10] that he often saw in the Cathedral.

---

[7] Some of the family's rural properties had vineyards. In Tinqueux and Trois-Puits, they owned three houses and vineyards. A document from 1663 records the sale of two vineyards located in Ay and Mareuil-sur-Ay by John Baptist's father, Louis de La Salle.

[8] The tonsure is a liturgical ceremony of initiation common in the Middle Ages and the *Ancien Régime*. In it, each ecclesiastical candidate cut off a piece of hair from the crown of his head to indicate his consecration to God and his entry into the clergy.

[9] At thirteen and fifteen years of age, respectively.

[10] The duties of a canon were related principally to public prayer, especially the daily chanting in the cathedral choir of the liturgy of the hours and the capitular celebration of the Eucharist. It was estimated that the financial remuneration received by the canons in the time of De La Salle was around 1,000 pounds per year.

At the age of fifteen, he was already one of them. A distant relative, Pierre Dozet, resigned his benefice as a canon of the Rheims Cathedral in favor of his young cousin John-Baptist. The most distinguished of the canons of this cathedral was Saint Bruno who went on to found the Grande Chartreuse monastery. It did not take long for John-Baptist to receive minor orders. I remember very lucidly that Saturday, March 17th, 1668. He looked so happy. The whole family joined him at that event.

John-Baptist de La Salle, at the age of 15. Canon of Reims Cathedral.

John-Baptist's passion for the Church and his obligations as a young canon of the Rheims Cathedral did not cause him to neglect his studies. He was still an excellent student. So much so that, at eighteen, he received his Master of Arts degree, *summa cum laude*.

You may wonder what that was all about. He had to go through the university curriculum with a medieval structure to receive that degree. He had to pass the curriculum of the seven traditional Liberal Arts. These were divided into two stages: the *trivium* (grammar, rhetoric, and logic) and the *quadrivium* (arithmetic, geometry, astronomy, and music). Once this period was completed, a young man could choose to study law, medicine, or theology, the most important careers at the time.

Unsurprisingly, John-Baptist chose to study theology and completed his first year at the University of Rheims. He deeply desired to prepare himself in the best possible way for his priestly vocation, which led him to move to Paris.

I remember the moment when we said goodbye to him, who, at the age of nineteen, was on his way to the Seminary of Saint Sulpice to continue his theological studies at the prestigious Sorbonne School of Theology, part of the University of Paris.

John-Baptist arrived in Paris in the autumn of 1670. Once he was settled in, we communicated through letters. In one of the first letters I received from him, he told me how happy he was at the Seminary of Saint Sulpice, where he was learning a lot from its formators, who were great teachers of holiness and prayer. He mentioned to me that he was discovering a spirituality centered on the person of Jesus Christ, which instilled him with great fervor.

He was in love with his vocation as a priest and felt called to represent Jesus Christ Himself in that capacity. He told me about the long hours of meditation and some references to that spirituality that marked him so much.

Old Church of Saint Sulpice.

He told me about the Society of Priests of Saint Sulpice and about the directors in charge of the Seminary: Father Louis Tronson, who probably had the greatest influence on him, and Father Heudon, with whom he used to talk about his life in the service of God. He was genuinely happy and, as expected, was doing very well in his studies.

Unfortunately, all that happiness was soon overshadowed as my beloved daughter, Nicole, mother of John-Baptist, suddenly passed away at the age of thirty-seven.

Only the Lord knows the pain that went through my heart after that loss. The memory of every scene in Nicole's life came back to me repeatedly.

I still cannot resign myself to the fact that the images of the wake and the burial of that day are part of this story. But I am convinced that God does not abandon His children and that His love is more significant than pain. I later shared that thought with John-Baptist, who could not be with us at the burial to say goodbye to his mother because of the distance that separated them. Imagine the pain he felt when he received the letter which contained such painful news.

John-Baptist has always been a young man with a lot of drive who is not intimidated by adversity, and even though the death of his mother was a very strong blow, he continued with his studies. Thus, he was able to complete the second year of theology. He had taken advantage of the holidays to return to Rheims and accompany the family through this difficult time. Then, he returned to Paris to start a new course. That was about October 18th, 1671.

It was during the second half of the year when another misfortune took place. This time, it was his father who died. It was only less than nine months since my daughter's death. It was another terrible blow to the family. Our mourning has lasted since that Saturday, April 9th, 1672.

That painful event changed John-Baptist's plans. On April 12th, he finished his studies at the Sorbonne; and on the 19th, he set out on his way back to Rheims. This time he returned with the responsibility to attend to family affairs. It was his father's will that he should be the executor of his will. The afternoon of that Saturday, April 23rd, had not yet arrived when he was put in charge of the situation. He became the guardian of his siblings and took care of the affairs of the house.

As executor he had to provide for the equitable distribution of the family inheritance, collect and manage the revenue from his father's property holdings, and assume his own role as head of the household. He was legally a minor, as the age of majority at the time was twenty-five years old.

Less than five months had passed since my grandson had returned from Paris, and now he was at the head of the family. Even so, he did not give up in the face of adversity. He continued to study theology in the evenings at the University of Rheims. A few months later, on June 11th, if memory serves me correctly, my grandson received the subdiaconate in Cambrai.

Sometime after that subdiaconal ordination, my grandchildren were separated into two groups. Marie and Jean-Remy came to live with me, while Jacques-Joseph, Jean-Louis, and Pierre stayed in their father's house with John-Baptist. Rose-Marie had already entered the convent.

When I look at John-Baptist today, I see a young man who has rapidly matured with the onslaught of life. The untimely death of his parents forced him to make changes in his plans, but his priestly vocation remained intact. That intelligent, bright-eyed boy now emerged as a man of God, determined to do the will of the One who had called him. I know that in those days, he intended to exchange his canonry for a parish; but, in that, he was unsuccessful.

His dream of becoming a priest would soon come true. I no longer remember why he went to Paris to be ordained a deacon. Still, I can tell you that that celebration took place in the chapel of the archbishop's palace on a Saturday, the eve of Palm Sunday. John-Baptist was twenty-four years old then. It did not take him much longer to obtain a licentiate in theology.

Those closest to John-Baptist witnessed the happiness expressed in his whole being on the day he was ordained a priest. It was Holy Saturday in 1678. All Rheims was celebrating because one of its sons received the sacrament to lead many on the path of faith. I cannot contain my emotions as I reflect on that beautiful celebration. My grandson had achieved his dream, his goal.

I remember, that as a child, he wondered what God had prepared for his life. He was very convinced that he wanted to hear God's voice. This fact reveals to me that today, being already a priest in love with his vocation, he continues to search for meaning ... to remain attentive to God's will.

As far as I am concerned, I continue to pray for him and for each of his Brothers. I cannot hide the pride I feel for my grandson. On these cold winter evenings, I sometimes wonder: Where will the Lord lead him?

Perrette Lespagnol Moët

Texts Consulted for the Writing of This Chapter

- Darnton, Robert. *The Great Cat Massacre and Other Episodes in French Cultural History*. New York: Basic Books, 1984.

- Deville, Raymond. *The French School of Spirituality: An Introduction and Reader*. Translated by Agnes Cunningham. Pittsburgh: Duquesne University Press, 1994.

- Gallego FSC, Saturnino. *The Life and Thought of John Baptist de La Salle* (vol. 1). Translated by Richard M. Orona FSC. Napa, CA: Lasallian Resource Center, tbd.

- Valladolid FSC, José Maria. *Lasallian Chronology*. Lasalliana (no. 31). Rome: FSC, 1994.

Hopeful Visits

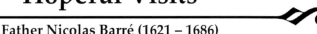

Father Nicolas Barré (1621 – 1686)

Rouen 1670

Father Nicolas Barré.

My name is Nicolas Barré. I am a religious priest of the Order of Minims, which is so named because we seek to make humility and penance a life option. We were founded by Saint Francis of Paola around 1474. Two years ago, I was elected superior of the convent of Rouen. I would like to share with you two visits that have been very important in my life because they were full of hope for God's favorites.

Both visits were from great friends. The first of these was that of Nicolas Roland. I remember that, while I was waiting for it, I was re-reading a text that was quite bold and beautiful at the same time. It was the *"Notices on the Necessity of Christian Schools for the Religious Instruction of the Poor,"* written by a priest named Charles Démia, a man committed to the cause of catechesis and the education of the poor. With great wisdom, he wrote his "Notices" to the Magistrates of Lyon.

I had been thinking about a startling passage:

To correct as many disorders as exist, and to reform the towns and provinces in a Christian way, there is no other way than to establish schools for the instruction of poor children. In them, with the fear of God and good morals, they will be taught to write, read, and calculate, by means of good teachers who will teach them these things and easily prepare them for work in most trades and arts.

Many priests, religious, and laity committed to the education of the poor of our time agree on this line of thought. The vast majority of the Catholic faithful in France in this century are mired in profound religious ignorance. And as if this were not enough, Calvin's[11] followers have made a great catechetical effort to instruct their followers.

Father Charles Demiá.

---

[11] Jean Calvin (1509-1534) was a very influential French theologian and lawyer of the Reformed Church initiated by Martin Luther (1483-1546). While carrying out his theological studies at the Sorbonne University in Paris, he had to flee to the south of France, following a controversy that arose at said university. Calvin was decisive in the establishment of the Reformed Church in Switzerland, first, and then in France. The followers of Calvin in France were called *"Huguenots."* After having been persecuted as heretics, and after the Wars of Religion fought in the kingdoms of France and Navarre between 1562 and 1598, the Reformed Church enjoyed a certain religious freedom in France through the Edict of Nantes (1598), signed by Henry IV.

De la Salle came into contact with the French catechetical-school movement when the edict of Nantes was still in force, which was revoked by Louis XIV, through the Edict of Fontainebleau, in 1685. This edict promulgated that, in France, only the Catholic religion was allowed.

11

Fortunately, the Holy Spirit always assists His Church in troubled times, raising up men and women of proven virtue to bring about authentic renewal. In the area of catechesis, I would like to mention some who see the formation of priests as a key to change. This is the case of Adrien Bourdoise, founder of the Seminary of Saint Nicolas du Chardonnet, and Jean-Jacques Olier, founder of the Society of Priests of Saint-Sulpice. In their seminaries, in addition to living a profound spirituality centered on the person of Jesus Christ, future priests are formed with special dedication to catechesis.

Characters who marked French spirituality and ecclesial life. Among them are St. John Eudes, St. Vincent de Paul, Cardinal de Bérulle, Mme, Acarie, St. Francis de Sales, Jean-Jaques Olier, St. John-Baptist de La Salle, among others.

But you know that the need for religious instruction is accompanied by many other needs at this time when poverty is rampant everywhere. This situation was experienced more closely by Vincent de Paul and Louise de Marillac, who took the catechesis of the poorest very seriously both in the cities and, particularly, in the countryside, where they carried out the so-called "rural missions."

The list could go on with Jean Eudes and many others, but I only mention these friends who, with their fidelity to the Spirit, have been able to gather around them other men and women to live generously the mission of proclaiming Jesus Christ in catechesis. I have no doubt that they sanctify themselves by their painstaking work on behalf of the sanctification of others, to the extent that their dedication to the poor is, for them, a duty, and a task.

The case of Nicolas Roland is no different. He is a young priest and canon of the Cathedral of Rheims, an indefatigable and big-hearted preacher, passionate about catechesis and the education of the poor. For some time now, the education of poor children in charity schools had us working together. He was preaching Lenten sermons in Rouen. I distinctly remember that fleeting visit. So much so that I can even transcribe our conversation:

Barré: Good morning, Father! How are the Lenten sermons going?

Roland: Good morning, Father Barré! You will know that these moments are always an opportunity to deepen our faith, through simplicity in life and generous dedication to others.

Barré: That is right! You told me in your last letter that you had an important matter to talk about. What is it?

Roland: I would like to make a specific request. Send some of the Sisters formed by you to Rheims so that they may begin work in our city like what they are carrying out here in Rouen. You know well the need for Christian instruction for the poor girls of Rheims. How good it would be for them to be educated in Christian schools!

Barré: It's true. I imagine that in almost every city the situation is just as urgent. I believe that there is a real possibility for some Sisters to go to Rheims, for I am certain that being under your protection, they will do great good for our Church. If everything goes as one can hope, I think they could reach their destination by the end of October or, at the latest, the end of the year.

Roland: Truly, children are more in need than adults. We have much to learn from them who, in their simplicity, take little care of themselves and are not attached to worldly things. As for the Sisters, rest assured that I will do everything in my power to make things go well.

Barré: May the Lord bless you, Father Roland! May the people of Rouen benefit from these Lenten sermons.

Roland: Thank you, Father Barré! Goodbye!

That visit on the fly, that conversation with Canon Roland, had, after some time, profound resonances in my life, for God's providence would open new horizons for the many poor boys and girls of Rheims.

Paris 1680

It has been ten years since I met my friend Nicolas Roland in the convent of Rouen. He has taken the care and accompaniment of the Sisters very seriously since their arrival in Rheims. So much so that, while taking care of two of them in their illness, he ended up catching typhus himself.[12] This disease put an end to his young life. But Roland's life, and work, was carried on by other people who followed his intuitions and apostolic zeal. Those Sisters whom I sent in October 1670 have grown in number and, with them, the apostolic reach of the schools for poor girls.

When Roland learned that the end of his earthly life was near, he appointed John-Baptist de La Salle and a young deacon named Nicolas Rogier as executors of his will. In that document, Roland entrusted them with the care and protection of the Sisters of the Child Jesus.

Recently ordained a priest, De La Salle learned of the death of his spiritual adviser. From that moment on, he took care of that community of Sisters with great diligence, both spiritually and materially. In fact, he was responsible for making representations to the authorities to confirm the legal establishment of the Sisters, to supervise their financial situation, and to make inventories of

---

[12] Typhus is an infectious and contagious disease that consists of a violent, delirious fever accompanied by small purple rashes on the skin. The medical name for the typhus is *exanthematous typhus*.

their assets. Undoubtedly, John-Baptist, in addition to being a priest with great spiritual depth, is a disciplined and intelligent young man who takes seriously the care of the Sisters of the Child Jesus.

I met John-Baptist years ago, after Nicolas Roland's death. Of all the times we have met, I remember in a special way that winter visit, close to Christmas, when he visited me at the convent in Paris next to the Royal Palace.

Not long before that visit, John-Baptist had embarked on the journey of the catechetical-school movement, accompanying a group of teachers who run schools for poor boys in Rheims. Our conversations revolved around how charity schools have become a divine instrument for the salvation of poor children. Evidently, such a conviction implied very bold choices in the lives of those committed to this apostolate. Well, the same thing was happening in the life of John Baptist. Little by little, the schools and the accompaniment of the teachers were opening new doors and closing others for him. New doors meant new options; and as you can imagine, De La Salle took the discernment of God's will very seriously.

Progressively he began to see that the accompaniment and organization of the community of teachers could not be done externally. All that remained was for him to be fully involved in that apostolate. Attempts to have them live together in a house under a set of regulations were not enough. That is why he took a bold step forward. He brought the teachers to take their meals at his house. Family friction began. Some of his relatives soon expressed their strong objections and displeasure with him.

That winter afternoon, after having participated in the solemn profession of his brother Jacques-Joseph in the Augustinian monastery, I met with John-Baptist. He was deeply discerning God's will in his life.

He felt a strong call from God to commit himself to a work that baffled him: laying the foundations of a community committed to the education and catechesis of poor children.

On that occasion, we talked about the importance of letting God do His work. Sizing up both the situation and John-Baptist, I responded with a direct and uncompromising challenge, that is, relying only on Providence in setting up the schools of charity. That is necessary for him and for the teachers he guided, that there should not be some kind of installation and material guarantees for the future. I remember saying to him, "Founded schools founder." We also discussed how much good is done to poor children who go to school free of charge to learn to read, write, and, above all, to know, love, and serve God from childhood to their whole lives. What I told him on that occasion was nothing more than that which I myself insisted upon with the Ladies of Saint Maur, a women's association under my direction in Rouen and Paris.

With more doubts than certainties, he said goodbye on that occasion. However, I was convinced that God would guide him in His own way, for John-Baptist is a faithful man. That visit was followed by others. As the years went by, I was able to witness the way God was working in De La Salle's life. As I mentioned before, John-Baptist took discernment very seriously and did not decide anything without being certain that he was doing God's will. He also sought the advice of his friends, among whom I have the pleasure of being counted. It was in this dynamic that an act of total detachment took place. When famine struck Rheims in the winter of 1684-1685, he distributed all his goods to the poor. The same can be said of his resignation from the canonry, after several twists and turns. A separate line deserves to note the step he has taken to a poor and radical lifestyle to accompany more intensely the community of teachers, who to date have consolidated themselves as a Community of Brothers: the Brothers of the Christian Schools.

As I write these lines, I can attest to the lucidity and courage that John-Baptist de La Salle had to constitute a Community of schoolteachers dedicated to the education and catechesis of poor boys. I admit that some of my contemporaries and I have tried to do the same without much progress. In John Baptist and the Community of the Brothers, it has been possible to concretize the desire of the school catechetical movement as a work consecrated to the Christian education of children.

When I look back on my encounters with my friends Roland and De La Salle, I can perceive in those visits the characteristic trait of the provident God who visits His people in times of distress.

Father Nicolas Barré

Texts Consulted for the Writing of This Chapter

- Barré, Nicolas. *Obras completas.* Edited by Thérèse Darras, M.-T. Flourez, and M. Toulouse & translated by M. Brandoly, M. Gelpi, and P. Tarazaga. Barcelona: Hermanas del Niño Jesús, 1997.

- Flourez, Brigitte. *Better Than Light: Nicolas Barré, 1621-1686.* Translated by Helen M. Wynne. Singapore: Angsana Books, 1994.

- Gallego FSC, Saturnino. *The Life and Thought of John Baptist de La Salle* (vol. 1). Translated by Richard M. Orona FSC. Napa, CA: Lasallian Resource Center, tbd.

- Gill FSC, Pedro. *Las propuestas de Barré a La Salle y la redefinición de la Vida Consagrada en la modernidad. Un ejemplo de reflexión lasaliana desde el contexto espiritual del XVII francés.* Revista Digital de Investigación Lasallana. Rome: FSC, 2016. Pages 1-28.

- Poutet FSC, Yves. *Charles Démia (1637-1689).* Cahiers lasalliens 56. Rome: FSC, 1994.

- Sauvage FSC, Michel. *Catéchèse et Laïcat.* París: Ligel, 1962.

- Valladolid FSC, José Maria. *Lasallian Chronology.* Lasalliana (no. 31). Rome: FSC, 1994.

Winning a Brother for the Kingdom of God

Adrian Nyel (1621-1687)

I prepared that trip to Rheims well in advance. Neither the dreams of what God's providence had prepared for me there nor the optimism that the visit close to Christmas 1678 had generated in me could make me neglect the work of the General Hospice of Rouen. I was working there at the time recruiting young men to establish schools. For twenty-two years I have been an administrator of the General Hospice. There, in addition to classes, I dedicated myself to animating a community of educators. We call each other "Brothers" because we are Christians, and we consecrate ourselves (though without vows) to the education of the poor.

For, as you will see, there were many things to foresee before making the journey of which I am speaking: Who would remain in my place for the duration of what awaited me? What money would I live on as long as that journey was prolonged? Who would accompany me? The answers to these questions take time to prepare, and nothing should be left to chance. For about five or six months before leaving, I took care of training a teacher to replace me, as well as managing a life annuity that would allow me to cover my expenses in a stable way. My companion on the road was Christopher, a young and enthusiastic assistant whom I was training.

You may wonder why that trip was so special. Well, because it represented, not only for me but for other people, a project of expanding God's goodness to poor children through Christian and charitable schools.

This trip brought together the hopes and experiences of men and women who have dedicated their lives to the poor. Clergy and laity, men and women.

In fact, I was on my way to Rheims with two letters from Madame de Maillefer,[13] one to the superior of the Sisters of the Child Jesus, with whom we had been working for some time.

The other letter was addressed to Canon John-Baptist de La Salle who, after the death of our friend Father Nicolas Roland, was taking care of the temporal and spiritual needs of the Sisters. De La Salle was reputed to be a young priest and canon, extremely effective in handling legal matters and with a particularly deep spirituality...

---

[13] Born in Rheims, Jeanne Dubois, after her marriage to Pons de Maillefer, moved to Rouen, where she had two stages in her life: the first of a princely type, dedicated to luxuries and excesses, and marked by vanity, contempt for the poor and an extremely comfortable life. After the death of a beggar in her home, she converted and began another stage, diametrically opposed to the one she had led before. She did everything she could to be humiliated; she mortified herself and dedicated herself to the care of the poor, having chosen to be one of them; sometimes, even to the point of begging. In Rouen she had a reputation, first of all that she had gone mad after her conversion and, in the course of time, she was seen as a saint. Canon Jean-Baptiste Blain says of her that in the city of Rouen: "She was an example to the people in virtue, after having been an example in scandal. From a famous and well-known worldly woman, she became an illustrious penitent. After having spent the first years of her life in the most exaggerated luxury, in a lazy and dissolute life, and in all the excesses of boundless vanity, she repaired it all with generosity, with the many years spent in daily humiliations, in the practice of the mortifications most repugnant to nature, and in the continual exercise of works of charity" (Blain, vol. 1, pp. 64-65). Madame de Maillefer founded a school for poor girls at Darnetal. She is an important personage in the history of the popular Christian schools of Rouen and Rheims. She was linked to the pedagogical ideas and spirituality of Fathers Barré and Roland. It was she who financed Adrian Nyel's journey from Rouen to Rheims.

When we left for Rheims, winter was not yet over. Providence willed that our meeting with John-Baptist was a *kairos*, an opportune time in which God works.

It was at the door of the Convent of the Sisters of the Child Jesus that this story began, and I will keep in my heart forever. It was a plan of God made concrete that would be revealed to me step by step with the passage of time.

From that first moment, I could perceive in Father De La Salle a very kind and cordial man. He

Father John-Baptist de La Salle meets Adrian Nyel, at the entrance of the Convent of the Sisters of the Child Jesus.

offered us hospitality in his house, in order to evaluate together all the aspects of the challenge of opening a school for poor boys in Rheims. In fact, he consulted many influential and charitable people in the city until, finally, the counsel received was that the best alternative was the one offered by the parish of Saint Maurice. Their parish priest, Father Nicolas Dorigny, provided us with lodging and sustenance.

But that was not the end of the story, as the possibility of opening a second school in Rheims soon appeared, specifically in the parish of Saint Jacques. Through the superior of the Sisters of the Child Jesus, I came into contact with a widowed woman named Catherine Lévesque [Madame de Croyère] who was willing to donate the money needed for the opening of the school. The friendship cultivated with Father De La Salle meant that we found ourselves working together again on this nascent project. He himself met Mme. Lévesque, and the school opened in September 1679. Before long, it had more students than the first.

The task of training teachers and presiding over the community fell to me. The rectory already had more inhabitants. We went from two to five. The facilities of the rectory and the resources of Father Dorigny, the pastor, were not adequate to provide for the growing numbers. Father De La Salle at first paid the additional expenses out of his own pocket.

By December 1679, it was evident that a more permanent solution was needed. Once again, Father De La Salle rented a house for us near to his own. Not only that, he also took care to give us a brief set of rules that included the rhythms of prayer, schedules, and other aspects of life in common. Food was brought to us from his house.

Parish of Saint Maurice.

The turn of the year brought us good news. Another school was opened in the parish of Saint Symphorien, and two more teachers were incorporated. By then, De La Salle had already welcomed us into his home on a regular basis to share meals.

The project of Christian schools for the poor children of Rheims gradually encompassed the life of the new doctor of theology. There was a community of seven teachers, three schools and around 400 or 500 children. It did not take long for the opportunity to open yet another school to appear. This time in Guise, where I had to leave while Father De La Salle and the teachers were living a Holy Week experience that had a positive impact on everyone's spirits. I could feel the change on my return after this unsuccessful trip.

When the lease expired in June 1681, De La Salle took us to live with him in his house on the Rue Sainte Marguerite.

Despite the family difficulties this decision meant for him, we were able to enjoy the accompaniment and closeness of the charismatic priest during these times. It was about ten months of many good lessons.

The Christmas season brought with it the possibility of opening another school. This time in Rethel. Father De La Salle had sent me to discuss the matter; and having listened to the request of the parish priest, the municipality, and the Duke of Mazarin himself,[14] we took up residence with another master in the Queutelot house on the main street.

Armand-Charles de La Porte, Duke of Mazarin.

The joy that this opening had generated in me, however, contrasted with the disappointment caused by the desertion of some teachers in Rheims. Fortunately, others arrived who were better disposed to meet the challenges. Father De La Salle had gone to Rethel at the request of the Duke, as there also had been some problems surrounding that foundation.

---

[14] Basically, "Duke" was a European title of nobility of higher rank, with which kings showed gratitude to certain people. As for the Duke of Mazarin, who supported the works of Nyel and De La Salle, he held several noble titles. Armand-Charles de La Porte, Marquis de La Porte, La Meilleraye, Duke of Mayenne and who, by marrying Hortensia Mancini, becomes Duke of Mazarin. His wife was the niece of the famous Raimondo Mazzarino, an Italian cardinal, politician and diplomat, a key figure in the *Ancien Régime's* history, as he became head of government to Anne of Austria and Regent for King Louis XIV. He took charge of the young king's education until he came of age, and then was also his prime minister until his death.

Marie de Lorraine.

After those problems were resolved, the Guise project finally came to fruition. The Duchess Marie de Lorraine[15] had requested my presence for the opening of a school. I went there; and in June 1682, one more school was already operating. Thanks to the great work that Father De La Salle was doing in the training of teachers, we were able to count on two of them in Rethel to replace me.

In Guise, at the beginning, there were two of us; but the work was hard, and I needed an assistant. As there were no more teachers available, Father De La Salle temporarily sent me his brother Jean-Louis![16] However, he soon had to return to continue his studies at Saint Sulpice.

It was more than three years of joint work with Father De La Salle. In those days, he himself had already established himself as a reference for Christian schools. He had formed a stable community whose members decided to call themselves "Brothers." In addition, he himself was already receiving requests for the opening of schools. That is how the school in Château Porcien came to be. But, on the other hand, other requests also fell on me; such as that of Laon, which I had to open at the end of 1682 in the street "Behind the Church" of Saint Pierre.

---

[15] Marie de Lorraine (1674-1724) belonged by birth to the French aristocracy of the dynasty of the House of Lorraine, a duchy founded in the 11th century. After her marriage to King Anthony I of Monaco, she became Princess of Monaco.

[16] The eldest of the three sons who were under the guardianship of John-Baptist after the death of his parents. When John-Baptist took the masters to live in his house, Jean-Louis was the only one who consciously decided to live with his brother. In another episode, when John-Baptist resigned his canonry, the Chapter of Rheims wished Jean-Louis to succeed him in the post. However, John-Baptist resigned in favor of a lowly priest Jean Faubert to the family's great displeasure. Jean-Louis, however, was closest to his older brother's projects. Having studied at the Seminary of Saint-Sulpice, he was ordained a priest. On several occasions, he found himself linked to the nascent society of Christian schools in Paris.

For some time longer, until October 1685, I had to direct the schools of Laon and Guise, while Father De La Salle did the same with those of Rheims, Rethel, and Château Porcien. Then I had to return to Rouen, my place of origin; and the schools remained under the direction of Father De La Salle.

I know very well that all the paths traveled with the teachers, priests, religious men, and women with whom I have worked could lead to a lot of enthusiasm, passion, madness ... and bewilderment. Like the one provoked in my friend John-Baptist de La Salle, the doctor of theology, former canon of the cathedral of Rheims, now turned into a humble formator of teachers (of Brothers) after having distributed all his riches to the poor. I had traveled to Rheims to seek help to open a school for poor children, but the provident God caused me to gain a Brother so that the seeds of the Kingdom would germinate and grow through the schools.

As for me, in my old age, I remain as administrator of the schools of the poor, dependent on the General Hospice of Rouen. When I look at the road I have traveled, I can clearly see how God has guided me in my journey and has united me with others to Father De La Salle. I have dedicated my life to Christian schools, being an instrument in God's generous hands. Today I can calmly await God's final call, for I am certain that God's work will continue with the nascent community of the Brothers of the Christian Schools.

Adrian Nyel
April 1687

Texts Consulted for the Writing of This Chapter

- Blain, Jean-Baptiste. *The Life of John Baptist de La Salle, Founder of the Institute of the Brothers of the Christian Schools* (vol. 1). Translated by Richard Arnandez FSC and edited by Luke Salm FSC. Landover, MD: Lasallian Publications, 2000.

- Campos FSC, Miguel. *Itinerario evangélico de San Juan Bautista de La Salle.* Madrid: Bruño, 1980. [Cf. De La Salle: *A Founder as Pilgrim* by Edwin Bannon FSC. London: De La Salle Provincialate, 1988.]

- Gallego FSC, *The Life and Thought of John Baptist de La Salle* (vol. 1). Translated by Richard M. Orona FSC. Napa, CA: Lasallian Resource Center, tbd.

- Rodríguez Mancini FSC, Santiago. *Adrián Nyel: Cómplice del Dios sabio y suave.* Buenos Aires: La Salle Argentina – Paraguay, 2012.

- Valladolid FSC, José Maria. *Las cuatro primeras biografías de San Juan Bautista De La Salle* (vol. 1). Madrid: La Salle Ediciones, 2010.

- Valladolid FSC, José Maria. *Lasallian Chronology.* Lasalliana (no. 31). Rome: FSC, 1994.

Difficult (But Fruitful) Stretches

Brother Gabriel Drolin (1664-1733)

My name is Gabriel Drolin. I was born in Rheims on July 22, 1664. I was baptized in the Parish of Saint Jacques in my hometown. I am a Brother of the Christian Schools. I live now in the Auxonne community about 220 miles south of Rheims. I arrived here after having traveled many paths, of which I would like to tell you about some stages.

It all began in the early 1680s, when I was able to learn about the work that Canon John-Baptist de La Salle was beginning in the city. These were free schools run by communities of teachers. The human quality, the charisma, the ability to organize, and the piety of Father De La Salle were attracting many young people from Rheims, among whom I count myself.

I admit that his decision to distribute his fortune to the poor, giving them food, had touched me deeply. I joined the Community in 1684, following God's call to this vocation. If I am not mistaken, it was that same year in which I became a Brother of the Christian Schools that we adopted a uniform way of dressing.

That year was really difficult.

John-Baptist de La Salle distributing food to the poor.

The autumn and winter were even harsher than the previous year, and a terrible famine struck the whole kingdom. Rheims became "an immense asylum." Father De La Salle ended up spending his fortune distributing food, especially to children in the city's schools for the poor.

Those initial times for me were very fruitful. I worked in Laon, north of Rheims, with a Brother named Nicolas Bourlette. There came a time when we both fell ill. Brother Nicolas died at the age of twenty-four, the result of a continuous and violent fever. Father De La Salle had been at the funeral. He was accompanied by Brother Henri L'Heureux. Due to these circumstances, we did not start classes until November that year. It was around that time that I discovered another aspect of Father De La Salle. He spared no effort to come to the aid of the Brothers who were sick or in difficulty. On many occasions, he did this even at the cost of his own health. The care he lavished on the Community was everything to him. In this, perhaps, he found his most genuine vocation, to the point of dedicating his whole life and talents to it.

However, the fledgling Community was not without its threats. The expansion of the Christian schools reached as far as Paris, where Father De La Salle had lived as a student. There were people there who knew him and had asked him for Brothers for the charity schools.

Two Brothers accompanied Father John-Baptist. They arrived in the capital at the end of February 1688 and began their work in a school of the Saint Sulpice parish. The students there were taught how to manufacture fabrics for sale. The school, on the Rue Princesse, had about two hundred students and a lot of clutter. It was run by a priest who initiated a series of intrigues against Father De La Salle and the Brothers. There were questions raised about the work of the Brothers and the authority of Father John-Baptist as the head of the community, but the new parish priest cut them short.

This new parish priest, Henry Baudrand, requested the opening of a second school, on the Rue du Bac, near the Pont Royal. However, he wanted to introduce modifications to the dress of the Brothers.

Father De La Salle took this very seriously and wrote a *"Memoire"* [Memorandum]. In it, in addition to describing the habit and pointing out its usefulness, he defended the identity of our Community, which is "lay" but not "secular" or "clerical." We are laymen who do not aspire to a position either in the world or in the hierarchy of the Church, but rather exercise a new ministry. Together we conduct free schools for the children of artisans and the poor.

Habit of the Brothers of the Christian Schools.

Undoubtedly, that "Memoir" did not go down well with more than one person and produced a hardening of positions, especially on the part of the parish priest.

In the late 1690s and early 1700s, the Community faced total misery that sparked a crisis. Brothers fell ill, others died, others left the Community, others became discouraged. This made up part of the picture of what seemed like a fall from grace. The other part was completed by the attacks of the Masters of the Little Schools,[17] who proceeded to seize furniture and materials from the school on the Rue du Bac.

---

[17] These schools were usually presided over by a single teacher who would set up shop, often in his own home. The diocesan supervisor of schools (the *Chantre* of the cathedral) was responsible for maintaining standards, protecting the rights of the teachers, and designating the precise territorial boundaries assigned to each.

This involved a kind of legal back-and-forth, which even went all the way to the supreme court of justice in Paris. Added to all this was the crisis in Rheims, where there were many leaving and only a few were entering. Could things get worse? Yes. Toward the end of that year, 1690, Father De La Salle fell ill in Rheims, as did Brother Henri L'Heureux in Paris. However, without having fully recovered, Father De La Salle set off for Paris. When he arrived, Brother Henri had already died and been buried two days earlier. This deeply moved him. Father John-Baptist got sick again, to the point of being bedridden for more than a month.

Many thought that his end was near, but we were hopeful of an improvement with the help of Doctor Helvétius.[18]

When Father De La Salle finally recovered, he took a long time to reflect on all that was happening. He took a series of measures for our Community: to better prepare the Brothers, to maintain, by letter, monthly communication, to have healthier houses, to open a novitiate. He also

Doctor Johann Friedrich Helvétius.

determined that there would be no priests in the Society, no study of Latin, nor would its members exercise liturgical functions in the church. From then on, all his organizational talent would be devoted to cementing the Community from within.

---

[18] Johann Friedrich Schweitzer, nicknamed Helvétius, (1630-1709) also known as Johann Friedrich Helvétius. Of Swiss origin, he was a medical doctor and prolific writer. An outstanding student at the University of Harderwijk, he obtained his doctorate with a thesis on the plague. He discovered the medicinal use of ipecac, a South American plant abundant in Brazil and Colombia, to cure dysentery. The formula used by the doctor was sold exclusively to Louis XIV, but was revealed in 1688. Helvétius also dabbled in alchemy and botany.

He proceeded to rent a house with a vegetable garden in Vaugirard, on the outskirts of the capital. There we had the annual retreat during the month of September. The Brothers from all the schools attended: from Rheims, Laon, Guise, Rethel, and those of us who were in Paris. Undoubtedly, this helped a lot to renew the declining strength and spirit of the Community.

The young Brothers remained at Vaugirard, receiving formation with Father De La Salle, while the rest of us went back to school. The fruits of that prolonged retreat were many ... God had brought us together to conduct, together and by association, free schools for the poor. In this journey, we have truly become Brothers with a very strong human and affective bond. This is how I experienced and expressed it in a vow together with Father De La Salle and Nicolas Vuyart; and here is the text:

Most Holy Trinity, Father, Son, and Holy Spirit, prostrate with the most profound respect before your infinite and adorable majesty, we consecrate ourselves entirely to you to procure with all our efforts the establishment of the Society of the Christian Schools in the manner that will seem to us most agreeable to you and most advantageous to the said Society.

And for this purpose, I, John-Baptist de La Salle, priest, I, Nicolas Vuyart, and I, Gabriel Drolin, from now on and forever, and until the last surviving one of us or unto the complete establishment of the said Society, make the vow of association and union to bring about and maintain the said establishment, without being able to withdraw from this obligation even if only we three remained in the said Society and if we were obliged to beg for alms and to live on bread alone.

In view of which, we promise to do, all together and by common accord, everything that we shall think in conscience and regardless of any human consideration to be for the greater good of the said Society.

31

Done on this twenty-first day of November, feast of the Presentation of Our Lady, 1691. In testimony of which we have signed.

That act of faith and courage would mark my life forever. I know it also marked that of Father De La Salle. Vaugirard remained our place of renewal despite the difficulties that never ceased to exist. Radical poverty, difficulties with the ecclesial hierarchy, and legal problems continued their menacing presence, while Father De La Salle was preparing different texts for the animation of the Community.

Vaugirard's country house.

It was on Pentecost Sunday in the year 1694, when twelve Brothers were summoned for a retreat that lasted until June 6th.

In this framework of prayer and fraternity, we had made several agreements and unanimously approved our Rule.[19]

---

[19] The *Rule of the Brothers of the Christian Schools*, written by John Baptist de La Salle, were drafted by a process worthy of note. Basically, the *Rules* had their origin in the experience of the community life of those first teachers with whom John-Baptist lived since the Assembly of 1686. The Founder made it clear that it was up to the Brothers ultimately to approve the Rule he was proposing. In the drafting process, the Founder consulted prudent people and had the collaboration of several Brothers. In this vein, De La Salle put at the service of the nascent community his talent for building consensus, systematizing practices and synthesizing in a vital piece of writing the basis of the life of the community. A manuscript dating from 1705 is preserved in the city of Avignon, probably a copy of the one approved by the Assembly of 1694. Toward the end of the Founder's life, modifications were made to the Rule after the Assembly of 1717. This is the manuscript of 1718.

On the feast day of the Most Holy Trinity, Father De La Salle and these twelve principal Brothers made the first perpetual vows in the Institute. The vows obliged us to conduct the schools by association, to remain stable in the Society, to be ready to beg if necessary and to live on bread alone, and to obey the Superior, the directors, and the body of the Society.

After that beautiful gesture, Father De La Salle wanted us to elect a new Superior. A Brother. Despite his insistence, the choice fell on him unanimously on both occasions. He had only to obey … but we had to make it clear that after De La Salle, we would accept only a Brother as our Superior. Since then, several more Brothers have taken vows, but I cannot hide my joy at saying that amog them there was one of my own brothers. Yes, Gérard Drolin took his vows with Claude Fouques at Vaugirard, on the Feast of the Immaculate Conception in 1697.

The turn of the century brought with it a new mission. I was sent to Calais for a new work. I worked there for a couple of years, until I was asked to go to Rome. I was accompanied by my brother Gérard with the mission of founding a school. The year was 1702. We left in October and arrived the following month. There we were received and welcomed by Father Gualtieri, who helped us unconditionally. Unfortunately, my blood brother Gérard returned to France, as he was discouraged and unable to adapt. Subsequently, he withdrew from the Institute.

The Drolin Brothers leave for Rome with the
Founder's blessing.

In February 1703, our protector in Rome was appointed bishop of Vaison, near Avignon. As for me, I then had to live as best I could. Father De La Salle sent me money when he could, and I lived in a house of some pious people: first a sculptor, then a merchant, both French. It was not until 1705 that I was finally able to establish myself in Rome by running a school.

Actually, it was a "branch" of another school. During this time, I remained in contact with Father De La Salle by means of letters. By this means, I kept up to date with some of the latest developments in our Society. I was finally able in October 1709 to obtain a license to teach in one of the papal schools. I was entrusted with a papal school to serve about sixty students. I was able to communicate this happy news to Father De La Salle.

I was working in Rome until 1728. I learned of the death of our Founder, on the early morning of Good Friday 1719, from a letter written by Brother Barthélemy. It was hard for me not to have been able to be there. Father John-Baptist de La Salle was a dear friend, a Brother who lived and dedicated his life to his Brothers.

On the threshold of my being almost seventy years old, I have returned to France after twenty-six years of working in Rome. I live the twilight of my days with the serenity of someone who gave himself completely to fulfilling his commitment to the Society to the end. Often, I repeat the same phrase of our Founder: "I worship in all things the will of God in my regard."

Brother Gabriel Drolin
Auxonne, 1731

Texts Consulted for the Writing of This Chapter

- Arribas Jimeno, Siro. *La fascinante historia de la alquimia descrita por un científico moderno.* Oviedo: Universidad de Oviedo, 1991.

- Blain, Jean-Baptiste. *The Life of John Baptist de La Salle, Founder of the Institute of the Brothers of the Christian Schools* (book 1). Translated by Richard Arnandez FSC and edited by Luke Salm FSC. Landover, MD: Lasallian Publications, 2000.

- De La Salle, John-Baptist. "Memoir on the Habit" in *Rule and Foundational Documents by John Baptist de La Salle.* Translated and edited by Augustine Loes FSC and Ronald Isetti. Landover, MD: Lasallian Publications, 2002. Pages 181-191.

- De La Salle, John-Baptist. "Rule of 1705 and Rule of 1718" in *Rule and Foundational Documents by John Baptist de La Salle.* Translated and edited by Augustine Loes FSC and Ronald Isetti. Landover, MD: Lasallian Publications, 2002. Pages 13-146.

- De La Salle, John-Baptist. "The Heroic Vow" in *Rule and Foundational Documents by John Baptist de La Salle.* Translated and edited by Augustine Loes FSC and Ronald Isetti. Landover, MD: Lasallian Publications, 2002. Page 203.

- Gallego FSC, Saturnino. *The Life and Thought of John Baptist de La Salle* (vol. 1). Translated by Richard M. Orona FSC. Napa, CA: Lasallian Resource Center, tbd.

- Valladolid FSC, José Maria. *Lasallian Chronology.* Lasalliana (no. 31). Rome: FSC, 1994.

The Association That I Lived ...
and Lost

Nicolas Vuyart (1665-1719)

The Parisian autumn is getting cooler and cooler and the gusts of wind blow away the parched leaves that have fallen from the nearby trees. The gray of the afternoon is in keeping with the deep sadness that overwhelms me. I went for a short walk to lighten the weight of the disappointment I carry in my life because of my actions. The biblical image of the vine and the branches comes back again and again to my thoughts, as if it were a shadow that accompanies my steps. How is it possible to lose what you love so much because of bad decisions? How do you withstand external pressures and have the lucidity not to deviate from the path? Why are we sometimes obscured by our own weaknesses? How is it that I did not know how to see that the branches cannot live unless they are united to the vine?

I am Nicolas Vuyart, and I am here to tell you a painful story. I must confess that I have made mistakes for which I do not forgive myself. Today I have lost the association with my Brothers (the Brothers of the Christian Schools). It was perhaps because of the circumstances or the pressures of the moment, or the voices that sounded louder than that first call to the Society, or, perhaps, the search for security in money or people, that ended up separating me from the Community.

I identify myself with the youngest son in Luke's Gospel account, who, repenting of his mistakes and very ashamed, returns to the Father's house. I tried it too, and I was welcomed with open arms by Father John-Baptist de La Salle, who wanted and sought my re-incorporation into the Community. But it would not be that easy. I had the same resistance that the youngest son in the Gospel story had from his older brother. Some people advised Father John-Baptist against my return to the community.

I remember the day I joined the Community in Rheims. The project undertaken by Father De La Salle was in search of talented and godly teachers for his community. That was God's call for me; and in a short time, I was immersed in the mission that was entrusted to me. The first of these was to replace a great educator, Adrian Nyel, in the city of Rethel, in the Duchy of Mazarin.

The nascent community that served the Christian schools was not always well understood and was immersed in innumerable conflicts. In Rethel, for example, the school operated in the same place where we lived. Initially, everything was going very well, with the financial support of the Duke of Mazarin, Armand-Charles de La Porte; but a short time later, without much clarity as to the reason, this support was withdrawn. We were all left in great precariousness. Fortunately, thanks to the mediation of Father De La Salle, the support that had been lost would be restored, at least partially. Undoubtedly, he had many business skills.

After having been in Rethel, I returned to Rheims for a while, to finally leave for Paris, in a new foundation located on the Rue du Bac. That must have been at the beginning of the year 1690. It did not take long for problems to appear. This time it was a conflict with the Corporation of the Masters of the Little Schools of Paris, who, seeing their interests affected, attacked the schools of the Brothers.[20] First, they showed up at the school to seize our property. They took almost everything. They then filed a complaint against us[21] with the school supervisor[22] for the archdiocese of Paris, Father Claude Joly, who summoned the parties to settle the problem. In the absence of the Brothers, he proceeded to agree with the plaintiffs by closing our school. How uneasy all this was for us! Why so much viciousness? They accused us of receiving children from wealthy

Father Claude Joly.

families who should go to their schools and thereby causing them economic damage.

---

[20] The conflict comes amid intense activity and a growing proliferation of schools in Paris. In addition to the Little Schools, there were the schools of charity, dependent on the parish priests. In this landscape there were also the Writing Masters, who constituted a corporation with a fixed number of members, specialized in the writing of minutes. The schools run by the Brothers are considered among the charity schools, but the community does not depend on the parish priest, since it has its own structure and superior. The complexity of the coexistence of these institutions provoked legal reactions, as well as searches for legitimacy and limitations to the actions for each type of school. In this sense, the school supervisor for the archdiocese [the *Chantre*] of Paris, Claude Joly, had written a treatise that sought to bring some order to the conflict, *Traité historique des Ecoles épiscopales et écclesiastiques* (Paris: Chez François Muguet, 1679).

[21] The defendants are: John-Baptist de La Salle, Bernard Legentil and Nicolás Vuyart.

[22] In De La Salle's time, the *Chantre* was the name of an ecclesiastical dignity that designated the master singer of the cathedral. In some cases, the *Chantre* also had the right to impose penalties on clerics who committed a fault and to report them to the bishop if they did not change their behavior. The *Chantre* had among his responsibilities: the direction of the choir, the ceremonies of the Church, the Divine Office, authority over song and music. In addition, he had jurisdiction and acted as superior of the Little Schools in which grammar, reading, writing, arithmetic, service to the Church, and catechism are taught, as well as good morals and all that should be taught to young children.

For us, on the contrary, the purpose of our schools was to give a Christian education to poor children. They meet morning and evening under our direction; and in our schools we teach them to live well, instructing them in the mysteries of our holy religion, inspiring them with Christian maxims, and thus giving them the education that suits them. But all this seemed to be little understood by those who were against the Christian schools.

This first attack, many others would follow, was about to make us desist, except for the intervention of Father John-Baptist de La Salle. As was common in his course, the first thing he did in this circumstance was to place himself in God's hands, so that God could prepare the way to follow. As a community we made a silent pilgrimage to the Church of Our Lady of the Virtues, a very frequented place, about five miles from Paris. There, Father De La Salle celebrated Mass and we all received communion. After long hours of prayer and fasting, we returned renewed in the Spirit. But, as was also the usual procedure, Father De La Salle also consulted Father Baudrand, pastor and the school's owner, on the matter. The latter urged him to appeal to Parliament against the sentence passed by the *Chantre* [school supervisor], and much to his chagrin, he did so. The court ruled in favor of De La Salle and the Brothers.

The joy of that battle won would be short-lived, as our opponents again appealed the sentence that had been promulgated on March 18th. They took less than a month to pepper their accusations with false data. The Parliament summoned the representatives of the Masters of the Little Schools and Father John-Baptist de La Salle, Nicolas Vuyart, Bernard Legentil and the owner of the building of the school on the Rue du Bac, Mme. Jeanne Quesmont, to give a sentence on the case.

Father De La Salle had presented his entire defense in writing, justifying that our school *"is a school of charity"* and, therefore, nothing is charged in it; and if anyone is not poor, he already confesses his poverty by joining the poor.

Thank God, that ruling again favored us and those who had confiscated the furniture and materials of our school, had to return them. However, after battles fought, there are always wounds. At the end of that year, Father De La Salle fell ill at Rheims. As soon as he partially recovered, at the beginning of the following year, he walked to Paris, where this time illness forced him to stay in bed for a month and a half. To Father De La Salle's fragile health, other events were added that shook our Community: the death of Brother Henri L'Heureux, the scarcity of new vocations, the departure of some Brothers, the precarious conditions in which the communities were ... How can we read all this with the eyes of faith?

However, Father John-Baptist has always been a man who knew how to draw strength from weakness. That condition was propitious to make our Community grow from within, and he himself made several decisions as our Superior: monthly communication by letters, annual retreat, renting a house for the Brothers to rest, opening of a novitiate, etc.

Signatures on the Heroic Vow.

All of that strengthened us, no doubt, but it would not be enough for him. He considered it vital to associate with two other Brothers to sustain our Society, until the end of our lives, even if it meant that we lived on bread alone.

I had the honor of making that heroic vow[23] together with Father De La Salle and Brother Gabriel Drolin. It was a profound, spiritual, sublime, and emotional moment. We had formed a nucleus to sustain the Community of Christian schools; that work of God so necessary for the children of artisans and the poor.

---

[23] It took place on November 21, 1691.

40

After this great event, I returned to Rheims for a few years, where I was the superior of the free schools for boys. Then, around June 1694, we received the summons of Father De La Salle to make perpetual vows in Paris. This time, the Society of the Brothers of the Christian Schools was strengthened by twelve Brothers who consecrated their lives to the Holy Trinity in order to conduct together and by association, free schools...

I returned to Paris at the beginning of 1699. This time the project was a new teacher training program,[24] for those who had to teach in rural areas. Two years later, we rented a house in the parish of Saint Hippolyte, in the Saint Marcel neighborhood. It was there that the school and the long-awaited teacher-training school would operate. Unfortunately, there too I would progressively move away from the ideals of our Society...

Neighborhood near the Parish of Saint-Sulpice, Paris.

---

[24] The idea of a seminary where teachers are trained was not new. As early as 1684 there were negotiations between De La Salle and the Duke of Mazarin to open one in the city of Rethel, which did not materialize. The one in Rheims, did not long survive. The purpose was to train teachers for rural areas.

In spite of the above-mentioned problems, the schools operated by the Brothers in Paris had considerable success and a good number of students.[25]

On the other hand, the human quality of Father De La Salle and the zeal of the Brothers aroused in other parish priests the desire to have a school for their own parishes. As a result of the friendship between Father John-Baptist and the parish priest of the Church of Saint Hippolyte, Michel Lebreton, the project for the school in the suburban neighborhood of Saint Marcel was born. I was sent there along with Brother Gervais. The good functioning of the school excited Father Lebreton, and he soon asked Father De La Salle for other Brothers to serve rural schools.

After a fruitful dialogue, that request led to the creation and opening of a teacher-training program for rural lay teachers. Basically, the teachers who came to be trained had to lead the same rhythm of life as we did and develop the same competencies of our ministry. The program, in terms of basic knowledge, included reading and writing well, arithmetic, and plainsong. As far as the concrete work of the teacher was concerned, the program taught how to deal with the children's different personalities and the methods to be used in a classroom with children of different ages and abilities in subjects as varied as reading and arithmetic. Obviously, the rural world differed from the urban world and several changes had to be made in methods. This was true, above all, when it came to reading, as many in the countryside considered it useless.

To carry out the project, a financing plan had to be considered. Father Lebreton secured a house for the Brothers from a devout layman on the Rue de l'Ourcine.

---

[25] According to the data of "Situation of the schools of the parish of Saint-Sulpice on December 1, 1698," there were 14 classes with about 1,000 students in Paris. Each class was conducted by a Brother.

A priest volunteered an annual sum a year, and some scholarships for teachers were established with the support of the Seminary of Saint Nicolas du Chardonnet.

The management of that work fell on me, and the undertaking was as successful as expected. Before long, it won my heart. Over the next two years, things took a normal course, until the problems returned with greater harshness.

The year 1702 marked the beginning of a stormy time that threatened to destroy everything that the Society of the Brothers of the Christian Schools had built up to that point. It all began with the mistreatment of novices by their director. The two novices turned to the parish priest of Saint Sulpice. The parish priest, in turn, went to the archbishop accusing Father De La Salle of not governing well. As you will see, all the blame was placed on Father De La Salle, to such an extent that he was deposed as Superior of the Brothers; and the archbishop placed Father Bricot as our superior.

Obviously, we did not accept that. The Brothers' refusal was strong at first; and despite repeated attempts to reach a Solomonic solution, things did not work out. Father Bricot, shortly after being appointed superior of the house of Paris, desisted from taking the helm and did not return to the Grande Maison. Throughout this process, Father De La Salle always maintained a conciliatory attitude toward ecclesiastical superiors. In return, he received only silence and indifference.

That unstable situation was a threat to our schools. How could we cope? Schools were at risk, and Father De La Salle was much questioned. These circumstances led Father Lebreton to consider it appropriate to make me the holder of his inheritance, in order to safeguard the educational work of the parish from other petty interests that might come from the curia. He had bet on me, knowing that I was very close to Father De La Salle. Father Lebreton died on March 9, 1703.

In addition to the uncertainty that hung over our Society, it was impossible to continue occupying the Grande Maison; and this led some Brothers of the community to move the following year to a smaller house in the faubourg Saint Antoine, on the Rue de Charonne. A school was opened there, with a placard that read: *"Frères des Écoles chrétiennes"* [Brothers of the Christian Schools]. A Sunday School also began operating in the same place, with an increasing number of students coming from all neighborhoods. And here is the beginning of another storm: the problem with the Writing Masters.[26]

This guild, through its trustee, Louis Lambert, initiated a complaint against Father De La Salle at the beginning of February 1704. He did so in the presence of the Lieutenant General of the Châtelet.[27] Soon after, the complaint had its effects. The police authorities seized the school on the Rue de Charonne. Benches, tables, books, and all teaching materials were taken. They also ripped off the placard on the front of the school. The school on Rue de Charonne ceased to function.

---

[26] The Writing Masters constituted a powerful guild of professional scribes under the protection of the king and the Parliament at the time. Their principal function was to verify the writings, signatures, accounts, and court records and to maintain the quality of penmanship in official documents. Admission came only after a long and difficult apprenticeship. A formal oath to preserve high standards of writing was taken by those who were admitted. They were continually feuding with the Masters of the Little Schools in an attempt to preserve their monopoly on the teaching of writing. In their view, the schoolteachers should restrict themselves to teaching reading only. The corporation had been established in Paris by a royal edict on October 16, 1570, following a case of forgery of the signature of King Charles IX of France. These privileges were still in force at the time of De La Salle.

[27] Justice in the *Ancien Régime* is characterized by its great complexity in terms of its institutional organization and, above all, by the confusion of its powers. For example, Parliaments had broad powers. Not only did they dispense justice and enforce the rules of law, but they also controlled the activities of the police and intervened in legislation, through the promulgation of regulations. The commissioners of the Châtelet in Paris were in charge of functions that placed them as auxiliaries of justice to settle rather particular cases.

After these events, the Châtelet summoned Father De La Salle to appear before the authorities. He made no move to defend himself. The sentence imposed a fine on him and the express order to teach only poor children who were certified as such. As if this were not enough, a week later the new *Chantre*, Father Perrochel, agreed with the Masters of the Little Schools and forbade Father De La Salle to have schools without his authorization. The case did not stop there, as the litigation reached the Parliament and continued its formal course thanks to a lawyer hired by Father De La Salle.

On the other hand, the quarrel with the Writing Masters did not cease. They attacked the Community again, and this time, they did so with greater force, filing a nominal complaint against Father De La Salle and eighteen other Brothers. My name as well as that of Brother Gervais was also on the list. The sentence was not long in coming. It imposed fines on Father De La Salle and every Brother listed.

The storm settled in our house and caused us a lot of concern, as well as on the parish priests of the Saint Marcel neighborhood.[28] The questions assailed my existence as if they were arrows hurled at my body. What should I do in that circumstance? How should we deal with this problem? How could we save the teacher-training program and the school? Would the school and the training of rural teachers perish, and with it the efforts and memory of dear Father Lebreton? It all seemed like a dead end.

On August 29th of that fateful year, 1704, my resistance was finally broken. By means of the judgment, we were condemned along with Father De La Salle to pay the Writing Masters impossible fines and compensations. The sentence was posted on the door of our school.

---

[28] The successors of Father Michel Lebreton were Fathers De Vougez, parish priest of Saint Martin, and Father Ravillar, parish priest of Saint Hippolyte.

In addition to the names of Father De La Salle, Brother Gervais and myself, the list also included the names of the pastors of Saint Martin and Saint Hippolyte. This time with an even more explicit prohibition. We could not form a community until the Society obtained Letters Patent. This was an almost impossible goal.

In my desperation, I felt I had to make a decision. At that time, I could only see two alternatives: remain in the Society of the Brothers of the Christian Schools, disobeying a court order, or try to save the school and the teacher-training program of rural teachers in the Saint Marcel neighborhood. After all, we had the inheritance left by Father Lebreton. I ended up opting for the second alternative, even though it meant withdrawing from the Community, renouncing association with the Brothers, and denying any link with Father De La Salle.

I went too far. I also gave up the habit and asked for a dispensation from the vows. But in spite of the uneasiness that the situation caused me, the zeal for those needy children of the neighborhood and the teachers who were being formed in the program continued to inspire my life. It was also the end of the path traveled with Brother Gervais who, for similar reasons, also separated himself from the community. However, he soon returned to it.

As time went by, things did not get better. Sustaining the school and the teacher-training program became impossible because the donations and support of the priests ceased. They stopped sending candidates. The project eventually fell apart. These circumstances made me realize the mistake I had made in separating myself from the Society.

As I told you at the beginning of this story, I wanted to go back to the Brothers. Father John-Baptist would have welcomed me with open arms, but others had read my actions as a great betrayal of the Community's mission.

I keep walking through the fallen leaves. What else do I have to tell you? Perhaps, despite the mistake made, which some will interpret as greed, attachment to people or projects, search for security, there are options that are unyielding. Mine, as long as I have the strength left, will continue to give the best of myself in favor of the school in the faubourg Saint Marcel.[29]

It's getting dark. The walk has come to an end.

Nicolas Vuyart
Paris, faubourg Saint Marcel, autumn 1704

---

[29] Nicolás Vuyart remained committed to the school in the Saint Marcel neighborhood for fifteen more years, almost the end of his life.

Texts Consulted for the Writing of This Chapter

- Campos FSC, Miguel. *Itinerario evangélico de San Juan Bautista De La Salle.* Madrid: Bruño, 1980. [Cf. De La Salle: A Founder as Pilgrim by Edwin Bannon FSC. London: De La Salle Provincialate, 1988.]

- Gallego FSC, Saturnino. *The Life and Thought of John Baptist de La Salle* (vol. 1). Translated by Richard M. Orona FSC. Napa, CA: Lasallian Resource Center, tbd.

- Joly, Claude. *Traitté historique des Ecoles episcopales & ecclesiastiques.* París: Chez François Muguet, 1679.

- Ministère de la Justice. *La justice sous la monarchie. L'Ancien Régime se caractérise par la diversité et la multiplicité du paysage judiciaire* (2007).
  [Obtained from Ministère de la Justice: http://www.justice.gouv.fr]

- Rigault, Georges. *History of the Institute of the Brothers of the Christian Schools: The Religious and Educational Work of Saint John Baptist de La Salle* (vol. 1). Translated by S. Edmond Dolan FSC and edited by Gerard Rummery FSC [https://lasallianresources.org]

- Sauvage FSC, Michel. *Catéchèse et Laïcat.* París: Ligel, 1962.
- Valladolid FSC, José Maria. *Las cuatro primeras biografías de San Juan Bautista De La Salle* (vol. 1). Madrid: La Salle Ediciones, 2010.

- Valladolid FSC, José Maria. *Lasallian Chronology.* Lasalliana (no. 31). Rome: FSC, 1994.

Letters for the Road

Brother Hubert (1683-1759)[30]

To embrace the life as a Brother has been a great challenge for me from the very beginning. The actions of the Brothers and Father De La Salle on behalf of the poor children of Rheims has had an impact on my life from an early age. I received the Lord's call to join this Society; and at the age of seventeen, I traveled with a friend named Clément to begin my novitiate in Paris. That Monday, April 20, 1700, was full of dreams and expectations, but also full of challenges.

During the novitiate, among the many things we learned, there was the Rule that was to govern our lives. Since 1694, the one used in my time as a novice has been approved. There was a specific section in it that referred to, what I will call, the writing of letters:

> *The Brothers will write every two months to the Brother Superior of the Institute, according to the Directory. The Brother Director will write every month, giving an account, for the first month, of his conduct and of the articles referring to regularity; and the second, of the Brothers and the schools. Brothers who need to write will join with the Brother Director when he gives an account of his conduct.*

---

[30] Brother Hubert (Gilles Gérard) entered the Institute in 1700. "At least six letters written by De La Salle to Hubert were preserved by Hubert … In 1717, he was one of the sixteen directors who attended the General Chapter at which Brother Barthélemy was elected Superior." He also attended the General Chapters of 1720, 1725, 1734, 1745, and 1751. He had been "director of at least seven communities over a period of fifty years."

As you see, there was a regular practice of writing letters between the Brothers and Father De La Salle, our Superior, in those days.

I cherish the letters I have received from him, for in them there was always a word of encouragement and guidance for all aspects of life. From time to time, I am accustomed to re-reading them, because our vocation is always unfolding and the ministry of the Brother is revitalized day by day. In addition, one can see how God is leading our lives with the passage of time as well as seeing how our life is anchored in the concrete.

Part of the manuscript of the Rule.

Today is one of those days in which it is possible for me to give a brief account of the path I have traveled with the accompaniment of Father De La Salle through his letters. As I re-read them, I try to put together ideas, teachings, and advice.

The work of accompanying a Brother in his personal growth has been a care that Father De La Salle has taken very seriously. Looking at the letter dated May 5, 1702, when I was a young Brother, I can read his insistence on renouncing my personal whims in order to allow myself to be guided by the Brother Director. In it he told me that the main virtue to which I should apply myself was obedience, because in it the will of God was manifested. I admit that this has been an aspect of my life that has particularly cost me a great deal, for in the letter of June 1, 1706, Father De La Salle again insists on this. Given my inexperience and the heavy responsibility of directing schools, Father De La Salle writes a letter filled with specific advice. Here are some lines that resonate as important to me in the letters:

> *Always have God in view in what you do; this is important if your actions are to be done in a Christian manner. [...]*

Indeed you can do no better than entrust yourself entirely to your superiors. [...] Tell me everything you feel you want to about your conduct, and I will try to help you. [...] There is nothing I hope for more in offering you advice than to put your mind at rest regarding the things you write to me about.

By that time, the Society had already entrusted me with the direction of two schools and the community in Laon. The challenge of looking after the community was enormous, since I had the great responsibility of setting an example for the other Brothers. This is something that cost me a lot because of my restless spirit. Perhaps I would like to have all the tools available to lead a whole life consecrated to God, but the concrete always pulls from the ideal and entangles us with our limitations.

On several occasions Father De la Salle exhorted me to act prudently, with restraint, soberly and obediently. Anytime. Anywhere. In the way we talk, the way we laugh, the way we behave. It was, finally, a matter of renouncing oneself in order to make room for the work of the Spirit of God. This, for me, meant regulating conversations inside and outside the house, keeping an eye on thoughts, whims, and inclinations, and watching over attitudes, especially those that led me to act condescendingly.

All of the above was aimed at the development of a spiritual life that is true and pleasing to God. This was the end that Father De La Salle had in mind. That is why he insisted a lot on application to prayer and its method, as one of the first precautions I had to take as a Brother.

In the letter of January 30, 1708, he told me that it was necessary to do violence to myself in order to reject the inopportune thoughts that come to mind, because they prevent us from doing prayer well. Attracting God's blessings is closely related to the care and correct application of interior prayer.[31]

---

[31] De La Salle composed a method of interior prayer for the Brothers. An abridged version can be found in the *Collection of Various Short Treatises* and another more developed version in the *Explanation of the Method of Interior Prayer*.

Growing in the spiritual life has become for me a long road of personal sacrifices, because it needs training our senses to be always attentive to the presence of God.[32] Particularly, it requires a singular way of looking at our actions; that is, to have God's eye on actions and to look at them as God would look at them.[33]

On the other hand, Father De La Salle constantly exhorted people to abandon themselves to God's will[34] and to never miss

---

[32] In the *Explanation of the Method of Interior Prayer*, De La Salle develops various modes of recalling God's presence. In other texts, such as the *Meditations for Sundays and the Principal Feasts*, other ways of recalling God's presence can be followed.

[33] In the *Collection of Various Short Treatises*, De La Salle explains what the spirit of this Institute consists of and refers to the expression "with an eye on God." The practice is presented in a question-and-answer format: (a) *What is it to do nothing except with an eye on God?* To pay attention to God when doing something, and to have God as the beginning and the end of everything you do; (b) *What does it mean to put your attention on God when you do something?* Think about God's presence today; (c) *What does it mean to have God as the principle of all that is done?* To consider God as the first author and mover of what is done, and to execute it only as if allowing oneself to be guided by His divine Spirit; (d) *What does it mean to have God at the end of all that is done?* Do everything for the glory of God, and solely for the purpose of pleasing Him.

[34] On God's will, we can read in the *Collection of Various Short Treatises*: (a) *What must be done to obey in everything only the commands and will of God?* Three things must be done: (i) recognize and worship God's commands and will in everything; (ii) conduct and control oneself in all things according to the commands and will of God; (iii) do not perform works except in order to accomplish the commands and will of God; (b) *What does it mean to recognize in everything the commands and will of God?* To be well persuaded and penetrated that there is nothing in which God's will is not fulfilled; (c) *What is it to worship God, or His commands and will, in all things?* To worship Him in all that exists, and in all the events of this life, particularly in those that happen to us, because God wills or permits them through love for us and for our own greater good; (d) *What is it to conduct oneself and regulate oneself in all things by the commands and will of God?* To take God's orders and will as the rule of all our whole conduct; (e) *What sign can one give that one takes God's will as the rule of all conduct, when we live subject to a Rule and are dependent on a Superior?* Acting only out of submission to the Rule and out of obedience to the Superior, with the intention of obeying God and fulfilling His holy will.

spiritual reading. On several occasions, he encouraged me not to give up on my vocation.

As I said before, Father De La Salle placed his trust in me from early on. First, he put me in charge of the school and then in charge of the community. Fortunately, I was always able to count on his support and practical advice to guide community life; and although it was not always easy for me, I found in his words the encouragement to act according to God's will.

As I re-read some of the letters, I can recall all those situations that I have gone through with my confreres. Some of them even make me laugh when I remember them. At other times, they remind me of difficult moments of community and coexistence.

As director, I was to watch over the conduct of the Brothers, in accordance with what was established in our Rule. In this, Father De La Salle insisted a lot on regularity.[35] While it is true that the efforts to remain regular were considerable, there was almost never a lack of situations that broke the daily order of the house.

---

[35] De La Salle has an extensive development on this subject in his writings. In Chapter XVI of the Rule, he elaborates on some points that condense his thinking on regularity: (a) the foundation of regularity is God's commandments, summed up in love of God and neighbor: (b) if regularity is separated from the observance of these two commandments it is quite useless to salvation; (c) regularity is established in communities to make it easier for their members to observe God's commandments. For example, silence, respect for one's superior, reserve in regard to the world, modesty, recollection, etc.; (d) the Brothers will love regularity and will regard it as the means of their sanctification: (i) because it helps them to observe the commandments; (ii) because it preserves them from temptations; and (iii) because God binds His graces to such observance in a special way; (e) regularity is the first support of communities. Irregularity is the first source of its destruction and the loss of its members; (f) that is why the rules of one's own Institute must be preferred to any other practices, unless they concern the commandments of God and of the Church; (g) consequently, each Brother must apply himself to the observance of regularity, desiring to do in all things and very exactly the will of God, which is manifested in them.

Regarding these, I did not hesitate to ask questions in my letters, to which Father De La Salle always replied with great delicacy and coherence.

Organization of the classroom in the Christian Schools.

Watching over our life together is not easy, and, sometimes, living together becomes complex. This touched me closely in the community of Guise, where it was difficult to unite wills and sustain the rituals of the community. In the letter of April 18, 1708, from Father De La Salle, I was once again drawn to the practice of regularity, which translated concretely for our community into ringing the bell on time, maintaining silence in the house, doing recess well, and that each Brother take care of what was entrusted to him. More particularly, he instructed me to be correct in rebuking the Brothers for their faults. I admit that this situation often distressed me a lot, but there was a conviction that it was a sure way to help them grow.

The Thursday Walk, in Gautier's work.

In the face of all that has been said and experienced, sometimes the question assails me: Why so much? And that's where the answer comes back to the school and the children, to the first vocation. In this, Father De La Salle always had an exceptional clairvoyance. Already in that distant letter of 1702, he wrote to me that I should apply myself fundamentally to prayer and to the classroom, since these are the two main occupations of the Brother.

It is for the sake of children that it is worthwhile to overcome impatience, to keep silent, not to act impulsively. On these points, Father De La Salle insisted again in the letter of 1708:

"You will have no order in your class except to the extent that you remain without moving about without speaking. Be very careful not to hit school children, both with your hand and with anything."

School dismissal - Artwork by Augustin de Saint-Aubin.

The existence of a community that collaborates with God's saving plan is opportune, also for the good of children. Father De La Salle is clear about this and leads the communities of the Brothers and the schools toward this ideal. Ten years have passed since those years full of learning.

Perhaps, the difficulties of the road make the walk a little heavier. But I am certain that fidelity is possible in spite of one's own weaknesses. It is just a matter, as Father De La Salle writes, to abandon oneself to the will of God.

Brother Hubert
Guise, 1710

Texts Consulted for the Writing of This Chapter

- Campos FSC, Miguel. *Itinerario evangélico de San Juan Bautista De La Salle.* Madrid: Bruño, 1980. [Cf. De La Salle: *A Founder as Pilgrim* by Edwin Bannon FSC. London: De La Salle Provincialate, 1988.]

- De La Salle, John-Baptist. *Collection of Various Short Treatises.* Translated by William J. Battersby FSC and edited by Daniel Burke FSC. Landover, MD: Lasallian Publications, 1993.

- De La Salle, John-Baptist. *Explanation of the Method of Interior Prayer.* Translated by Richard Arnandez FSC and edited by Donald Mouton FSC. Landover, MD: Lasallian Publications, 1995.

- De La Salle, John-Baptist. *Meditations.* Translated by Richard Arnandez FSC and edited by Augustine Loes FSC and Francis Huether FSC. Landover, MD: Lasallian Publications, 1994.

- De La Salle, John-Baptist. "Rule of 1705 and Rule of 1718" in *Rule and Foundational Documents by John Baptist de La Salle.* Translated and edited by Augustine Loes FSC and Ronald Isetti. Landover, MD: Lasallian Publications, 2002. Pages 13-146.

- De La Salle, John-Baptist. *The Letters of John Baptist de La Salle.* Translated by Colman Molloy FSC and edited by Augustine Loes FSC. Romeoville, IL: Lasallian Publications, 1988.

- Gallego FSC, Saturnino. *The Life and Thought of John Baptist de La Salle* (vol. 1). Translated by Richard M. Orona FSC. Napa, CA: Lasallian Resource Center, tbd.

- Sauvage FSC, Michel. *Catéchèse et Laïcat*. París: Ligel, 1962.

- Sauvage FSC, Michel, and Miguel Campos FSC. *Announcing the Gospel to the Poor: The Spiritual Experience and Spiritual Teaching of Saint John Baptist de La Salle.* Translated by Mathew J. O'Connell. Romeoville, IL: Christian Brothers Conference, 1981.

- Valladolid FSC, José Maria. *Lasallian Chronology*. Lasalliana (no. 31). Rome: FSC, 1994.

The Other Side of The Story

Father Antoine Brenier (1651-1714)[36]

A long time has passed since those youthful years in the community of the Seminary of Saint Sulpice and classes at the Sorbonne. In that place, everything was oriented to the holiness of the seminarians and priests. Today it is a bit amusing for me to remember those healthy competitions that existed between us, whether for piety or for qualifications. The priestly vocation, so devalued in those days,[37] sought to reach its fullness at Saint Sulpice.

---

[36] We present here, as a kind of "antagonistic gaze" or "alternate look at things," a figure who is often called the "enemy" of De La Salle. He is a priest belonging to the "Society of the Priests of Saint Sulpice" who knows the Founder and the community of Brothers closely. His identity has been preserved by the first official Lasallian biographer [Canon Jean-Baptiste Blain] referring to him as "adversary," "rival," "enemy," or "persecutor." Even today, his identity is the subject of speculation. Some specialists maintain that the "enemy" is Father Joachim de La Chétardie, pastor of the parish of Saint-Sulpice in Paris, where the Brothers were in charge of four charity schools and a Sunday School. Brother Saturnino Gallego maintains, however, that he is Father Antoine Brenier, superior of the minor seminary of Angers, consultor of the Society of Saint-Sulpice, and later Visitor of the same. Here, we assume the figure of Brenier as the "enemy" of De La Salle, someone who has achieved an effect contrary to his good intentions toward the community of Brothers in Paris.

[37] "At that time, concern for the clergy was everywhere in France. Too many priests, lacking formation, without authentic spiritual life, often with many interests ... The picture was bleak" (cf. Deville).

Cardinal de Bérulle, Father Charles de Condren and Father Jean-Jacques Olier,[38] the latter was the founder of the Society of Saint-Sulpice to which I now belong, had devoted the best of their lives to restoring the state of the priesthood. Those of us who aspired to the priesthood had to be animated by a spiritual life marked by the apostolic spirit, the full meaning of religious worship, and a very solid interior life. All this had its center in deep communion with Jesus Christ, the Incarnate Word of God.

Father Jean-Jacques Olier.

There we were taught that the spiritual life of the priesthood should be nourished by the scriptures and constantly renewed through the Eucharist and prayer. Of course, devotion to the Virgin Mary and the apostles was also very important.

In the *Spiritual Directory of the Seminary of Saint Sulpice*, we can read:

> *The first and definitive goal of this Institute is to live totally for God in Christ Jesus Our Lord, so that the interior of His Son penetrates into the depths of our hearts and enables us to say with confidence what Saint Paul said about himself: "It is not I who live, but Christ who lives in me" (Gal 2:10). In all this will be the only hope and the only thought, and also the only exercise: to live the life of Christ interiorly and to manifest it by acts in our temporal deeds.*

---

[38] John Eudes's name is also added to these names to refer to "the big four" of the French School of Spirituality. De La Salle and Louis-Marie Grignion de Montfort also belong to this spiritual current, whose characteristic themes are theocentrism, mystical Christocentrism, the sovereignty of the Mother of God, and the exaltation of the priestly state (cf. Deville).

My formation in Sulpician spirituality made a deep impression on me. In the words of the Psalmist, "You are a priest forever according to the Order of Melchizedek" (Ps 109). From a very early age, I felt called by God to His service. At the age of ten, I was healed in an extraordinary way through the intervention of the Virgin Mary herself. How could I reject God's call to the priesthood?

I came to the Seminary of Saint Sulpice after graduating as a lawyer. There I met John-Baptist de La Salle, a native of Rheims, who, like many others, was in search of good priestly formation. We were companions for less than two years when the death of his father forced him to return to his hometown.

Church of Saint Sulpice.

In addition to being an excellent student, De La Salle was very enthusiastic about the catechetical practices that were given in the parish schools. A pious Sulpician priest named Father Jean-Jacques Baüyn oversaw these practices.

That apostolic and spiritual fervor led me to enter the *"Society of the Priests of Saint Sulpice"* in 1686; but out of humility, love, and respect for the priesthood, I asked to delay my ordination until the following year.

I had not seen De La Salle for a long time. I heard of him when, in 1683, he resigned the canonry and caused no small stir among the faithful of Rheims. I also learned that he was organizing a community of teachers who called themselves Brothers and that the Christian schools. The schools they conducted had already gone beyond the borders of Rheims.

Five years later they arrived in Paris to take charge of the school of the Parish of Saint Sulpice. That was a great joy for us. We knew of the great good that the schools and the Brothers did for poor children through the evangelization they carried out. And what better place to do this than your old home!

At that time, the superior of the Seminary and of the Society was Father Louis Tronson, who was very fond of De La Salle. The parish was run by Father de La Barmondière and his vicar, Father Baudrand. Father Compagnon, the priest in charge of the Parish's charity schools, was in our community in those days. Initially, he was the one who had suggested and arranged for De La Salle to take over the management of the school that is located on the Rue Princesse.

Father Compagnon had been somewhat upset because the deal was finally concluded with the parish priest and not with him. Thus, the Brothers took charge of the school under the orders of the parish priest. The internal leadership of the community of Brothers would be under the authority of De La Salle. Admittedly, the school picked up a lot with the arrival of these new teachers.

Shortly after Father Baudrand took over as the new parish priest, we learned of De La Salle's intransigence when he refused to accept the change of the Brother's habit. Truth be told, those men looked ridiculous in that outfit. Despite Father Baudrand's insistence, the request was not complied with. What's more, De La Salle wrote a document defending the habit the Brothers wore.

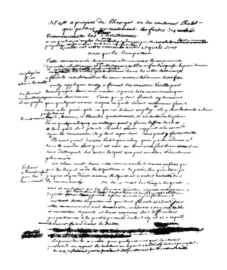

Manuscript *"Memoire on the Habit"*

At some point in the document, he argued about the inadvisability of the use of the ecclesiastical habit and the tonsure, because he asserted the Brothers do not have and will not have ecclesiastical studies, nor will they exercise any function in the church, nor will they wear the surplice.[39]

I ask myself: Where is the love for the priestly condition that had been instilled in us so much in the seminary? Why so much closure? Despite everything, the parish priest ended up not only giving in but also supporting the opening of yet another school in the parish. This one was on the Rue du Bac.

Admittedly, the work done by the Brothers in the schools was truly admirable – enough to generate envy from other contemporary educators.

---

[39] This text is the *"Memoir on the Habit."* De La Salle wrote the text in which, among other points, he described the habit used by the Brothers and explained why it was not advisable to change it. On this latter point, the Founder specifies: *"Changing the habit is a matter of importance in a community; hence, most religious communities take great care to avoid all circumstances that might lead to its alteration. In several communities the habit is prescribed not only to its shape and the quality of the material but also with respect to its length and breadth. All the dimensions are exactly indicated so that the habit will never be altered. The communities of religious priests that adopted at their foundation the clothing then in fashion, among other clerics, have steadfastly retained the original habit and have thereby ended up making it distinctive. For the past five years, this habit of the Brothers has been worn in five different towns, both in the diocese of Rheims and in that of Laon. There it is regarded as a decent and appropriate habit designed to keep the teachers true to the diligence and reserve proper to their state and profession and to invite the respect of their students and the esteem of other people, far more than the jackets they formerly wore. People have grown accustomed to this habit, and changing it would give rise to gossip, invite criticism for being faddish and frivolous, and induce superiors to bring back secular dress. The Brothers of the Christian Schools have been teaching in Paris for nearly two years in this same habit, and during that time no one has lodged any complaints about it except the parish priest of Saint Sulpice, who recently has spoken rather strongly on the matter. If this habit were objectionable, this should have been pointed out, it would seem, when the Brothers of the Christian Schools came to Paris and before they were employed in the schools there. They should have been told then that they would not be permitted to teach in this distinctive habit and that they would have to adopt one more commonly used. Then they would have had to decide what measures to take."*

But it is also true that De La Salle's pretensions as Superior were quite high, and he was ready to fight even in the courts. That was how he confronted the Masters of the Little Schools and the Writing Masters.

Another matter of concern was the Community. I have witnessed the austerity in which the Brothers lived. In some cases, they were too austere with themselves. I have seen them fall ill and become discouraged. Moreover, De La Salle himself was in mortal danger. He did not die thanks to the intervention of a great doctor, but the other Brothers did not suffer the same fate. Actually, I think that his abilities to lead a Community were not the most sensible. However, he always had the support of the community of Saint Sulpice.

A glimmer of hope was glimpsed when he opened a novitiate in Vaugirard, precisely in the place where the "Society of the Priests of Saint Sulpice" had taken its first steps. That place, on the outskirts of Paris, had welcomed some novices. Those years were rather bleak throughout France. A climatic disaster that lasted from November 1691 to May/June 1694 was followed by a war[40] that brought with it a demographic disaster, pestilence, and much famine.

Old Church of Vaugirard.

Around February 1696, the parish of Saint Sulpice received as its new parish priest Father Joachim de La Chétardie, a member of the Society.

---

[40] This is the so-called War of the Grand Alliance (1688-1697) that pitted France against the Grand Alliance, made up of the League of Augsburg and England.

Like his predecessor, he had a special affection for the Brother's Community and the work they did. This led him to open two more schools in the parish during his ministry with one on the Rue Placide. Before the opening of the latter, De La Salle had already moved the novitiate to what they called the Grande Maison closer to the parish. There began a very encouraging project: a Sunday School.

Father Joaquín de La Chétardie visits the Christian Schools.

Relations between the Brothers and the Sulpician community were always good. We knew each other, and there was trust. However, these enthusiastic and fervent men, in my opinion, were badly governed. De La Salle was arbitrary and obstinate.

Why had he not yet obtained the Letters Patent for that Community in need of acquiring its own property? Who had set him up as judge and Superior of it? What jurisdiction did he have over the Brothers? In fact, De La Salle's command as Superior was unclear. The schools depended on the parish priests, but the Brothers who worked in them owed obedience to a priest who did not have the lights to lead it. That was unacceptable. Many times, I have tried to bring them to their senses, but I have not been listened to. Even the parish priest would have liked to take over as ecclesiastical superior of the Community, to help them have a better organization, but he came up against De La Salle again and again, a man locked in his own judgment. Not only was his authority as the head of the Community questionable, but his administration was also dubious. Why were some of the new Brothers formed in Paris, with parish funds, sent to other cities? By what criteria?

Despite these inconsistencies, the parish priest, Father de La Chétardie, had entrusted De La Salle with the Sunday School. This type of school, common in the region of Flanders, was established for those young people under twenty years of age who, because of their life circumstances and manual trade, did not have time to go to school, but who, nevertheless, had Sundays and holidays free. In its early days, the Sunday School was a success. There were about two hundred young people, divided into different classes. There they learned to read, write, and do arithmetic, and, in some cases, also received classes in drawing, geometry, and knowledge of more advanced mathematics.

The curriculum was not only limited to the above-mentioned knowledge. There was also Christian formation received through the catechism and exhortations.

To be sure, Sunday School was a sure means of keeping many young people away from vice, disorder, games, vagrancy, and occasions of sin. It was also intended to awaken in them a taste for the arts, work, and a solid Christian life. In fact, the school was known as The Christian Sunday School.

However, once again, De La Salle's lack of tact in leading the Community could not prevent the Brothers who ran the Sunday School from quitting. That meant the collapse not only of the school but also of the illusions of many young people who had only that opportunity to be trained. It was an unfortunate episode.

In his defense, De La Salle argued that no Brother wanted to be formed to replace those who left, for fear that the studies they would undertake would lead them down the same path of desertion. He had given that plea in writing to the parish priest. Neither Father de La Chétardie nor the undersigned could believe that this letter came from the Brothers. Most likely, as he has done with the previous parish priest, De La Salle has written another manifesto justifying his customary closed-mindedness.

The situation caused great discontent in the parish community. What we used to celebrate with joy slowly turned into grey episodes. The man we once saw as a priest skilled in governing and training new Christian teachers is now a shadow of questioning.

For the priests who conform to the Society of Saint Sulpice, listening to those who come to us in search of a spiritual word is very important. Especially if they are priests or seminarians, not excluding those who have embraced religious or lay life.

The Rule of the Society makes it explicit: "*Even if they come many times a day to interrupt it, the community will welcome them with the same charity, it will listen to them with the same patience, it will answer them with the same gentleness as if it had only this one business in the world.*"[41]

In this spirit, I received a couple of novices who came to complain about the mistreatment they had received in the novitiate of the Grande Maison. On the first occasion, the defendant was Brother Michel, novice director; and the second time the accusation fell on his counterpart, Brother Ponce, director of the community on the Rue Princesse, in whose charge they were during a period of the internship in that school. The treatment and punishments received by the novices were disproportionate; and they could be attributable to the directives of the person who was at the head of that Community.

The collapse of the Sunday School, the dissatisfaction of some Brothers with their vocation, the divisions in the community, the mistreatment of the novices, the precarious conditions of the communities, and the inability of the Superior to govern made a sum that deserved special attention on the part of the Society.

---

[41] The quoted passage is found in point 6 of the *Constitutions of the Society of the Fathers of Saint Sulpice* and is based on point 12 of the *Collection of Rules of the Society of Saint Sulpice*.

I myself was responsible for drafting a report on these points. When I presented it to Cardinal Noailles,[42] I took care to provide as much detail as I could. The above-mentioned novices agreed with what I wrote. This action led to an investigation of the Community, which partly confirmed what had already been written.

Cardinal Louis Antoine de Noailles.

Father Edme Pirot, vicar-general, prepared a negative report in which, once again, the harshness of De La Salle's life and the penances practiced in his communities were revealed. In this way, it became clear that the Community of the Brothers of the Christian Schools must have another ecclesiastical superior. This was also understood by the Cardinal, who communicated his decision to dismiss De La Salle after a courtesy visit that the latter had paid him.

Although De La Salle's attitude toward his Eminence was one of absolute submission and acceptance, it did not take long to motivate a rebellion of the Brothers against this decision.

Everything seemed to be going smoothly at the meeting convened by Father Pirot to announce the decision taken. De La Salle had summoned most of the Brothers of Paris to the Grande Maison. As soon as it became known that Father Bricot was to be the new Superior of the Community, the Brothers reacted in the worst way. They rudely refused to accept the edict of the archbishop.

---

[42] Louis-Antoine de Noailles (1651–1729), who was to become Cardinal-Archbishop of Paris, was appointed bishop of Cahors in 1679 and of Châlons in 1680. In 1695 he was promoted to the archbishopric of Paris. In 1700 he was made a cardinal at the suggestion of Louis XIV. He was rector of the Sorbonne in 1710. He also was involved in the Jansenist controversy.

No one expected that those silent and modest men would be able to raise their voices to say, "We already have a Superior freely chosen by us." They even showed a document that said:

> *Having associated ourselves with John-Baptist de La Salle, priest, to conduct together and by association the free schools by the vows we made yesterday, we acknowledge that, in consequence of our vows and the association we have contracted for them, we have elected as Superior John-Baptist de La Salle. It is our intention that after him, in the future and forever, there will be no one received among us, nor elected as Superior, who is a priest or who has received Holy Orders; and that we will not even have or admit any Superior who is not associated and has taken vows like us, and like all those who will hereafter associate with us.*[43]

Again, it was to be expected that De La Salle would have used his writing skills to draft such a text and persuade the Brothers to sign it. In addition, they appealed to the cardinal and threatened to withdraw from the schools of Paris. "If you want to put a Superior, bring the inferiors as well; we are leaving," some shouted to Father Pirot and Father Bricot. That episode was unfortunate. It was an act of rebellion, undoubtedly incited by those who clung to their status as directors.

After that embarrassing situation, in which De La Salle tried in vain to appease the tempers that he himself had inflamed, a group of Brothers went to see the parish priest, with the firm conviction of abandoning the schools in case the deposition was not reversed. He promised them a prompt solution. Others came to me.

---

[43] The act dates from June 7, 1694. De La Salle and twelve Brothers previously held a retreat from May 30th to June 6th, after which they made their perpetual vows of obedience, association, and stability. They then discussed the issue of the election of a new Superior. Twice consecutively and unanimously, De La Salle was elected. This gathering is also considered to be the first General Chapter of the Institute.

I could not hide from them my disapproval of this act of rebellion or my disappointment in it. Those feelings opened a rift that distanced me from the Community. The way I understood things, there was no turning back; and I considered a solution to this problem almost impossible.

In their attempt to make me understand what had happened, those Brothers left me a copy of their Rule,[44] which they would not be willing to change for any reason. In vain I tried to find in it some aggravating clause about mortification, fasting, or extreme punishment. I was able to read in it some points, however, that did catch my attention:

> *There will be no corporal mortification, that is the rule in this Institute; however, there will be abstinence from meat on Saturdays from Christmas until the feast of the Purification, as well as on the Monday and Tuesday before Lent, except on journeys.*

> *The Brothers will all fast together on Friday, one day of the week. On this day, six ounces of bread will be given to each Brother for the collation, with dessert as on the fast days of the Church.*

However, in my opinion, this did not agree with what the Brothers were experiencing. Perhaps the paragraph about the Brother Director, which says, "The Brother Director may, however, impose greater penances, according to the needs of the Brothers and the seriousness of their faults," justifies what happened to the novices; but even so, I consider that the Community needed a different leader and a Superior.

De La Salle also moved his pieces. He went to see Cardinal Noailles to ask forgiveness for what had happened. As far as I could tell, and as might be expected, he was received coldly and distantly.

---

[44] The excerpts quoted in the text correspond to Chapter 5 of the *Rule of the Brothers of the Christian Schools*, which is entitled "On the Exercises of Humility and Mortification to be Practiced in this Institute."

Things would not have ended well had it not been for the intervention of the parish priest Father de La Chétardie. In an act of great diplomatic skill, the Cardinal sent Father Madot to the Grande Maison. He conversed informally with the Brothers; and after several hours, he finally made a concrete proposal. De La Salle would remain the Superior, while Father Bricot would be in the condition of external ecclesiastical superior and would visit only once a month.

However, this was not enough for the Brothers, who tightened their grip on requiring the conditions to be written and signed. In addition, they demanded that the Rule of their Institute not be altered. Evidently, this was not to the liking of any of the priests involved in this episode. But, in the end, it seems to have been the only way to make peace.

Unfortunately, Father Bricot soon declined his new position. After his official presentation at the Grande Maison, he only returned there once more after three months, and then never returned again. I imagine that it was not easy for him to take care of a Community based on a Rule that was alien to him, with consolidated practices, with its own pedagogy and language. Evidently, he could not have directed this story in any other way.

I would have liked to have been appointed for this purpose, for I knew the details of the Community much more closely. It could have done far greater good to those men who courageously took up the task of evangelizing through the Christian schools; but the unity they showed after that episode and their fidelity to De La Salle made him accept resignedly what had happened. Still, I would rather see a man with few lights for the government at the head of the Community than the collapse of the schools.

Relations between De La Salle and the community of Saint Sulpice were never the same after that episode, although the Sunday School has resurfaced thanks to a Brother who was formed for that endeavor.

The rift that opened up after the rebellion of the Brothers also translated into physical distance. As soon as the lease on the Grande Maison ended, the owners put it up for sale.

De La Salle wanted to buy it, but the most sensible thing to do was to distance himself. As a result, the community moved to the Rue Charonne, where they opened another Sunday School, with a large turnout of young people from various neighborhoods in the area. And, as if marking a territory of their own, they placed a sign in front of the house that read: *Frères des Écoles Chrétiennes* [Brothers of the Christian Schools].

As expected, the lack of wisdom to move within the legal margins soon led to new problems for De La Salle and his Community. After an achieved apparent calm, quarrels with other Parisian educators soon multiplied.

In vain, I tried to make them see that other options were possible. Rather, the results backfired; and I ended up being singled out by the Community.

But certain situations are clarified only with the passage of time. Imagining the future of the Community

Work produced by a writing master - [caligrapher]

of the Brothers of the Christian Schools, led by John-Baptist de La Salle, I do not foresee serene times. But only time will tell.

Father Antoine Brenier,
who is called "the enemy"

72

Texts Consulted for the Writing of This Chapter

- Baudet, Jacques. "Joachim de la Chétardie (1636-1714): Curé de Saint-Sulpice" in BMSAHC, n. 1 (January-March 1968), pages 22-59.

- Campos FSC, Miguel. *Itinerario evangélico de San Juan Bautista De La Salle*. Madrid: Bruño, 1980. [Cf. De La Salle: *A Founder as Pilgrim* by Edwin Bannon FSC. London: De La Salle Provincialate, 1988.]

- De La Salle, John-Baptist. "Memoir on the Habit" in *Rule and Foundational Documents by John Baptist de La Salle*. Translated and edited by Augustine Loes FSC and Ronald Isetti. Landover, MD: Lasallian Publications, 2002. Pages 181-191.

- Deville, Raymond. *The French School of Spirituality: An Introduction and Reader*. Translated by Agnes Cunningham. Pittsburgh: Duquesne University Press, 1994.

- Gallego FSC, Saturnino. *The Life and Thought of John Baptist de La Salle* (vol. 1). Translated by Richard M. Orona FSC. Napa, CA: Lasallian Resource Center, tbd.

- Sauvage FSC, Michel. "For a Better Understanding of Lasallian Association" in AXIS: *Journal of Lasallian Higher Education 5*, no. 2 (2014), pp. 93-115.
- Society of the Priests of Saint Sulpice. *Constitutions of the Society of the Priests of Saint Sulpice*. Paris, 2005.

- Valladolid FSC, José Maria. *Las cuatro primeras biografías de San Juan Bautista De La Salle* (vol. 1). Madrid: La Salle Ediciones, 2010.

- Valladolid FSC, José Maria. *Lasallian Chronology*. Lasalliana (no. 31). Rome: FSC, 1994.

The Language of God

Sister Louise Hours (1646-1727)[45]

The mornings in Parménie dress in their best clothes in spring. The landscape allows you to contemplate the power of creation in all its splendor. The chirping of greenfinches and other birds fills the air while the sun stains the mountains with colors. At the shrine of Our Lady of the Cross, activities begin early. Every detail is important to attend to the pilgrims who come to these mountains in search of peace and a word of encouragement.

I am here along with other pious women who help me with this task. It has been years since that time when, as a young shepherdess, while praying over the ruins of a chapel on the site, I received a message from the Lord to rebuild it. Since then, I have been working and praying tirelessly. This is how Parménie soon became a spiritual reference point in this area.[46]

Sister Louise of Parménie.

The site has a permanent chaplain in charge of celebrations and confessions, and today, a rather peculiar pilgrim arrived.

---

[45] Louise Hours, a pious laywoman, is familiarly referred to, by Lasallians, as Sister [Soeur] Louise of Parménie.

[46] Parménie is about twenty-two miles southeast of Grenoble.

He is a priest, well into his years, with signs of infirmities in his health and spirit. He has come to do a retreat for a couple of weeks. Alerted by the chaplain, Father Yse de Saléon,[47] I was waiting for him.

"Welcome to Parménie, Father De La Salle," I said. The priest from Rheims, seemingly a man of few words, thanked me kindly for the reception and told me that he could sense in my greeting the charitable and humble tone of a woman given to God. After a short rest and prayer in the chapel, he went to one of the places outdoors where it was possible to appreciate the valley and the horizon. I accompanied him there. "That God is everywhere, there is no doubt," he managed to say; "but here ...." My gaze was, also, fixed on the horizon. "Here," he added, "you could certainly be able to make the words of the psalmist your own: 'O Lord our God, how wonderful is your name in all the earth!'"[48] A long silence followed this brief exchange, during which both of us seemed to tune into the same spiritual frequency. Days went by, and that harmony made a few more words between us possible.

Parménie.

---

[47] Father Yse de Saléon was an acquaintance of John-Baptist de La Salle.
[48] Cf. Psalm 8:2.

"I must confess to you, Sister Louise," the pilgrim said one day, "that I have come here carrying a very heavy burden. I have been traveling roads that have not been easy. Never before have I had so many doubts. The One in whom I have placed all my trust, lately, does not say anything to me."

A deep uneasiness was stirring within him. He seemed to be feeling, deep down in his being, that he had been betrayed. In fact, he had apparently been enduring pressures that gradually broke his spirit. Attacks by the Writing Masters against his schools, he told me, had begun in 1703; and these were, then, followed by those of the Masters of the Little Schools, who were supported by the *Chantre* [school supervisor]. Then, there were the problems of the Paris community...

The latter was what seemed to have hurt him the most. The Brothers in the Paris area, fed up with struggles or simply disoriented, had ended up accepting an external ecclesiastical superior,[49] contrary to what had been agreed upon by the Brothers in the 1694 Assembly.

Apparently, the same had been done in other communities of the North. How could this have happened? He felt that, at least implicitly, this led to the loss of identity of the body of the Society and to the denial of himself as Superior. "Rest, Father," I counseled. "Let this holy place, these mountains, relieve you of your physical[50] and spiritual pains." I tried to reply in a gentle tone.

---

[49] In 1702, De La Salle had been deposed as Superior of the Brothers in Paris by Cardinal Noailles, and Father Bricot had been appointed in his place. After a manifestation of disagreement by the Brothers, the matter had apparently been resolved with the abandonment of functions by the one who had been appointed by the Cardinal as superior. However, in the absence of the Founder, this time it was Brother Barthélemy who asked for ecclesiastical superiors for the communities.

[50] De La Salle, at the age of sixty-three, suffered from the ailments of age (rheumatism); and he was subjected to a treatment based on very intense heat. In addition, he was also teaching in class, replacing the Brother Director of the Grenoble community who had been sent by him on business to Paris.

The following days passed between the silence of the retreat he was making and his long moments of prayer. Only when the time was right was there room for a somewhat longer dialogue between the two of us. Like the one we had that afternoon, when Father De La Salle was finally able to express his sorrow in more detail. "I have put all my strength and devoted almost my entire existence into doing God's will, into doing His work," he told me. "However, everything now seems to indicate that I must step aside so that the work can walk on its own. More than an instrument with which He builds, I am now an obstacle to the advancement of God's will. But, all in all, my love for Him remains unwavering."

His slow words seemed to carry a heaviness in themselves. They reflected his uneasiness in the face of great existential uncertainty. "I am little less than an outlaw," he added very quietly as if a great cloak of shame covered him.

"An unjust condemnation weighs upon me.[51] Evidence which should have proven my innocence has been used against me, and I have been betrayed by people I trusted greatly."

---

[51] In 1712, De La Salle was convicted twice by the courts in a case concerning the opening of a seminary in Paris for the training of lay teachers for schools in the countryside. After the insistent proposals of a young man named Jean-Charles Clément, the Founder had finally agreed to advance a part of the money for the purchase of the house where the seminary would operate. The other part was provided by Louis Rogier, a lawyer friend of Clément, who was listed as the buyer. The young Clément, who because he was not yet twenty-five years old was still considered a minor, signed an acknowledgment of the debt. The seminary began operating in April 1709. However, in 1711, Doctor Julien Clément, father of the young man in question, filed a lawsuit against De La Salle, seeking to keep the house and expel its occupants from it. The legal issue led to two rulings: the first, dated February 17th, rescinded the contracts signed by Jean-Charles Clément; and a second, dated May 31st, obliged De La Salle: (a) to forfeit the money he had advanced; (b) to reimburse Clément for the maintenance of the student teachers; and (c) to pay the costs of the trial. The sentence of the courts read: "We forbid the said Monsieur De La Salle to demand from minors similar acts or money, as well as to use any such procedures."

At these words, Father De La Salle fell silent again. After an interval, I tried to put into words my own experiences. "God's ways are as difficult as they are perplexing. His work involves carrying heavy crosses. And this is as true for both enlightened people as for ignorant people who are attentive to His voice.

I myself have been imprisoned a couple of times, called a thief, a faker, a madwoman, a vagabond."[52]

Although my words probably did not bring any theological newness for him, De La Salle told me they were a living reminder of a recent Gospel passage he had come across in prayer, which had initially appeared vague and very painful. He noted that perhaps it was now an opportune moment to retrace his steps and look back over it all once again in his own mind.

Perhaps, he mused, he should have chosen to stay in the Grande Chartreuse monastery, where he had only recently visited, for he always felt a peculiar attraction to seclusion and silence. The memory and example of Saint Bruno, one of the founders of the Grande Chartreuse and a former canon like himself of the Rheims Cathedral, inspired him deeply. Then, again, he wondered if perhaps he should stay at Parménie, in this new place which was quickly becoming so precious to him.

Monastery of the Grande Chartreuse.

He was beginning to find himself very comfortable, confessing and preaching to the pilgrims; and he was enjoying the spring air and the peace of the mountains.

---

[52] Sister [Soeur] Louise, a humble shepherdess, was illiterate. She had undertaken the reconstruction of the chapel in Parménie and went all over the region asking for money for this. In that process, she suffered all kinds of ill-treatment and was even imprisoned. After that place became too small for the number of people who came there, she planned a building expansion, for which she again undertook a collection facing similar problems.

In spite of the problems of the communities linked to the Sulpician parish of Paris, in spite of the attacks of the Writing Masters and the Masters of the Little Schools, in spite of the judicial sentences, in spite of the ill-treatment he had recently received in Marseilles,[53] and in spite of the trials of old age and illness and tiredness and many other bitter pills ... recently ... in nearby Grenoble, where the sun also rises so gloriously behind the mountains, a visit to a community of younger Brothers had rekindled in him the flame of fraternal love.

Yes, De La Salle had been very comfortable in Grenoble. So much so that he stayed there for a few months, enjoying the peace of the community, the solitude of the house, and the secluded life he led there. The director was Brother Jean, one of the twelve Brothers who made their final vows with him in 1694.

It was in that community that he stayed before these days of retreat here on the hill of Parménie. And, yet, something brought him back with us, a second time, to this place of pilgrims.[54]

---

[53] This really was a very sad episode. According to Brother Jean-Louis Schneider, it was a complex and, to an extent, a generational conflict that not only dealt with cultural aspects (the South of France, a bi-lingual reality, was quite different from the North) but also with differences in the Brothers' mentality regarding obedience and authority. The tension affected the local community and the novitiate that was about to open. The Founder was accused of being very strict with the novices, concerning practices of piety and penitence. The novitiate ended up closing because of departures and a lack of candidates. The Brothers of Marseille said to De La Salle: "Everything here was going along fine until you came along. Why do you come here to destroy the whole enterprise instead of helping to make it grow?"

[54] Perhaps this visit was a return of favors to his friend Father Yse de Saleón, whom he went to replace in his capacity as chaplain of the retreat house in Parménie.

This time, for a slightly longer stay than his previous visit.[55] "Sister Louise," he confessed to me one morning, "I wish I could spend the rest of my days here, in solitude, to think only of God and to pray for the conversion of sinners." Trying to keep my serenity and being transparent and simple, I replied: "That is not God's will. You must not abandon the family of which God has made you the father. Work is its portion; it is necessary to persevere to the end of your days, uniting, as you have begun, the life of Magdalene with that of Martha."[56]

Claude-François Dulac de Montisambert.

Those words remained floating in the air while the old pilgrim had a lump in his throat, which led to a profound silence. A shared silence, I could say. It was on another one of those sunny spring days that a young pilgrim named Claude-François, a former soldier, arrived in Parménie with Father Yse de Saléon. He had come to the mountains to discern his vocation; and he encountered Father De La Salle, whom he asked for accompaniment.

---

[55] There were no lack of people who spread the story that De La Salle stayed for life in Parménie. According to a biographer of Sister Louise, the Benedictine monk Théodore Bellanger (from Parménie), De La Salle had such fond memories of the shrine on the hill that he stayed there for life, confessing and guiding pilgrims.

[56] In ancient times, reference was made to the biblical text of Lk 10:38-42, which narrates Jesus' visit to the house of Martha and Mary, in associating both the active and the contemplative dimensions of religious life. Magdalene is mentioned here instead of Mary. Why? Most likely, this is a confusion of biblical personages. In addition, Sister Louise may have known that, just previously, De La Salle made a forty-day retreat in the convent of Saint-Maximin, located at the foot of the mountain of Sainte Baume. According to tradition, Mary Magdalene would have dedicated herself to penance after the resurrection of Jesus there.

It seemed that he'd attempted to try out a monastic vocation with the Capuchins and the Trappists but had been accepted by neither. What better test of solitude could be found than here with us in Parménie?

De La Salle was attentive in the accompaniment of the young man. Everything indicated earlier about Father De La Salle's own search seemed also valid for that of Claude-François. And, so, it came to be that Father De La Salle invited him to be a Brother! While De La Salle was accompaning the former soldier in his vocational discernment, God was apparently using Claude-François to do the same with the old priest.

No one was able to explain the reasons or circumstances very well. The truth is that one morning, Father De La Salle received a letter that seemed to answer the many questions that brought him to Parménie.

"I'm going back to Paris, Sister!" he said, with a countenance that radiated happiness. "Thank you for everything!" "Go with God, Father," I replied, knowing without doubt what God was doing with the pilgrim priest.

Once again, God had begun to communicate with Father De La Salle on the mountains; and I, a humble shepherdess, can understand how His love is manifested in the service of pilgrims, a young man with a military background going in search of his vocation, and an elderly priest, with a doctorate in theology, who found himself once again just a humble pilgrim on the journey.

"There they go," said one of my Sisters, as Father De La Salle and the young man departed.[57] "Blessed be God! Only His love is sure and will last for all eternity," I responded. Meanwhile, the sun continues its course and spreads its warm, luminous light over the mountains.

---

[57] The soldier was Claude-François Dulac of Montisambert, who in the Institute will receive the name of Brother Irénée and become a director of novices and Assistant to the Superior of the Institute.

In its wake, the flowers and meadows of Parménie are as resplendent as ever with bright colors; and Father De La Salle, too, as he re-begins his pilgrim journey, is a witness to God's glory at every moment.

Sister Louise

Texts Consulted for the Writing of This Chapter

- Alpago FSC, Bruno. (May 2018). *Los Clément y el Seminario de maestros para el campo de Saint Denis.* Asociados (18), 16-17.

- Bellanger, Théodore. *Soeur Louise: la pieuse bergère de Parmenie.* Paris: Des Bons Livres, 1857.

- Gallego FSC, Saturnino. *The Life and Thought of John Baptist de La Salle* (vol. 1). Translated by Richard M. Orona FSC. Napa, CA: Lasallian Resource Center, tbd.

- Schneider FSC, Jean-Louis. *The Rendez-Vous on the Hill: Parménie 1714-2014.* Translated by Terry Collins FSC. Paris: District de France, 2014.

- Valladolid FSC, José María. *Lasallian Chronology.* Lasalliana (no. 31). Rome: FSC, 1994.

- Valladolid FSC, José María. *Las cuatro primeras Biografías de San Juan Bautista de La Salle. Tomo IV. Índices de lugares, de personas, analítico y cronológico.* Madrid: La Salle Ediciones, 2010.

- Villalabeitia FSC, José Antonio. *"¿Qué pasó en Parmenia?"* in Unánimes 158 (2002), 5-16.

Master, Friend, Brother!

Brother Jean Jacquot (1672-1759)[58]

Remembering … there are some memories so pleasant that they are difficult to forget, no matter how much time passes. It has been a long time since some teachers arrived in Château-Porcien, my hometown. That was quite a novelty because these men were coming to open a school. It was not long before I was among the other children who attended it. I soon discovered that these men, who called themselves "Brothers," devoted their whole lives to the education of poor children. I was fascinated by their goodness of heart, care, and faith life. Even more so when Father De La Salle showed up. We all admired him.

Soon I was immersed in that world, where the experience of God lived in the daily life of the school. I also wanted to be a Brother. I applied to join the Society, but I was too young … only fourteen years old. So, I was admitted to the junior novitiate.

They gave me the habit; and with a heart full of happiness, in those young years, I did nothing but learn from the Brothers to pray, to teach, to love my vocation, and to put my life in God's hands.

---

[58] Brother Jean Jacquot entered the Institute in 1686 and was one of the twelve Brothers who pronounced vows with John-Baptist de La Salle in 1694. He was the director of the community in Grenoble from 1713 to 1715. When Brother Barthélemy "requested [in 1717] that two Brothers be elected to help him in the administration of the Institute, Jean was the first one elected as Assistant to the Superior."

The difficulties, which were many, did not diminish the power of the Spirit that lived and continues to live in our Society. Yes, moved by the Spirit, we knew how to weather the storms, and, together, we made our perpetual vows in 1694. I signed the formula of vows with eleven other Brothers at the age of twenty-one.

Act of election of the Founder as superior. Below left, the signature of Bro. Jean.

The school, the children, the Brothers, and the learning were the means by which God made me fall in love with His work.

After years of being in the classroom, I was entrusted with the role of Inspector, that is, to accompany the novice teachers in their teaching. This task was basically to watch over everything that happened in the school as far as the teachers and the children were concerned.

As an Inspector of Schools, I had to watch over the learning process of the children, i.e., indicate the time allocated to each class, agree with the teachers on when to change the lesson or class of the students and examine which students needed help or teaching materials to support their learning.[59]

---

[59] Transparencies, for example, will be given only to such students who are unable to write straight without lines. The Inspector of Schools and the teacher will examine those who may need them, and they will make the least possible use of them. A transparency is a sheet of paper with lines drawn across it at proper intervals. It is called a transparency because of where it is placed beneath the sheet upon which writing is to be done, the lines are visible through the paper and serve to guide the lines of writing. Each one of the writers were to have a sheet or two of coarse paper, which easily absorbs ink. To dry what is written without blotting it, they were to place the coarse paper over the page on which they have written. This coarse paper is, on account of the use made of it, called blotting paper. (Cf. The Conduct of the Christian Schools: Section 5: Transparencies and Blotting Paper.)

I was also to see to it that the rules and customs of the school were observed, i.e., to take care of order, discipline, and punctuality. This latter was so important that it became a necessary condition for admitting children to the school. Regarding the accompaniment of the novice teachers,[60] I had to help them to progress in the virtues of our ministry, the way they were to conduct themselves, in the world, and to advise them in all that has to do with the activities of the school. In short, I had to see to it that nothing was missing in the school regarding both the teachers and the children.

I could not neglect the smallest detail because the Work of God does not admit negligence, and requires the commitment of people wholly consecrated to Him. How can we keep quiet about this gift of God and not joyfully proclaim it to others?

However, where many of us happily found a total consecration to the God of Life through the Christian education of the children of artisans and the poor, others felt threatened in their petty interests. So, it was that Father De La Salle and our Society suffered attacks of various kinds on several occasions. Sometimes we were nominally denounced, as was the case at the time of the Writing Masters of Paris in June 1704.

My name was on the list of those denounced along with those of other Brothers.

The Christian school. The Founder and a Brother attentive to his teachings.

---

[60] Cf. *The Conduct of the Christian Schools*: Appendix A: Part Three: Duties of the Inspector of Schools contains three articles: (a) matters concerning school; (b) matters concerning teachers; and (c) matters concerning students.

On other occasions, the attacks were more violent, and our schools were even looted. But the ones who did the most damage, without a doubt, were those who tried to undermine the foundations of our Society. The subtle but profound onslaughts that threatened to destroy a unity that, for a period of time, led to a crack from within.

The sum of those blows eventually took its toll on Father De La Salle, who had to flee Paris because of legal problems with the Clément family. After a long and painful journey in the South, he eventually reached Grenoble. There we, in the community in Grenoble, received a tired, sick, and dejected man. We did everything we could to restore his health and spirits. He occupied a small place in the upper part of the house, which practically became his place of retreat and prayer. For him as well as for us, it was an opportune time to remember the foundational motivations and to renew affection and fraternity. He also devoted himself to correcting The Duties of a Christian to God, an important piece of writing for our schools and for our Society.

He was also able to indulge in a few short days of retreat at the Grande Chartreuse monastery.[61] Unfortunately, however, his rheumatic pains reappeared, and this time, with greater intensity. Happily, he was able to regain his health after undergoing painful and risky treatments.

For our community, it was very meaningful to watch over and go out of our way to protect the health of the one we consider our father.

While Grenoble suited Father De La Salle, the conditions of the Paris community continued to worry him greatly. He sent me there to gather detailed information about the situation. But what about the school that was in my care? I did not have to worry

---

[61] The monastery was founded by Saint Bruno, a canon of the Cathedral of Rheims. De La Salle, as a canon, occupied stall number twenty-one where Bruno also sat in the choir area of the chapel. The Founder had great admiration for this saint.

since he took charge himself, along with the other Brothers of the community.

I deeply admired this man who, at sixty-two years old, still had great energy to replace me as a teacher in the school and to take care of housework.

While in Paris, I was able to see that there was great bewilderment on the part of the other Brothers at the prolonged absence of Father De La Salle.[62] The feeling of not having a Superior hung in the air.

Brother Barthélemy, perhaps ill-advised, was departing from the foundational roots of our Society, directing each local community to ask the local bishop to appoint an ecclesiastical superior for the communities of Brothers in each diocese. Fortunately, there were

Staircase leading to the tower room occupied by the Founder during his stay in the community of Grenoble.

Brothers and other good people who warned about a possible schism in our Society; and the reactions were not long in coming.

Having appointed external ecclesiastical superiors during this period of the Founder's absence, the Brothers resolved that they should only deal with them on material matters, to have them as protectors of the community and convene, if necessary, a general assembly. The urgency of these times also led to the hastening of the procedures on the part of the Brothers to obtain the Letters Patent for the Institute.

The situation greatly perplexed Father De La Salle. Consequently, he decided to withdraw even more. He became silent so that God might speak to him. He headed out from our community in Grenoble for the hills of Parménie. Meanwhile, his adversaries were about to deal the final blow.

---

[62] An absence is also marked by silence and a break in correspondence.

They wanted to change the *Rule*[63] of the Institute. A theological conjuncture[64] and the intervention of some Brothers prevented what would have been the certain destruction of our Society.

Back in the community of Grenoble, having just returned from his retreat in Parménie, he told us about a letter he received while there. It was signed by the leading Brothers of Paris and other nearby communities. It read:

> *Monsieur, our very dear Father, We, the principal Brothers of the Christian Schools, having in view the greater glory of God, the good of the Church and that of our Society, consider that it is of the utmost importance that you should resume the conduct of God's holy work, which is also your own, since it has pleased the Lord to make use of you to establish it and guide it for so long a time.*

> *We are all convinced that God has given you the necessary grace and talents for the proper government of this new Society, which is of such great utility to the Church, and we acknowledge in all justice that you have in fact always guided it with much success and edification.*

---

[63] A proposal for changes in the structure of the Community was presented to Cardinal Noailles so that each local community would depend on the parish in which the school and the community were established, and each community would have its own novitiate to which novices would be admitted depending on the number of Brothers who were needed to teach. With this, there would no longer have been a single Superior or novitiate, nor would there have been any changes among communities. In short, there would no longer have been one Society, and each community would then have been a self-sufficient entity unto itself.

[64] At that time, controversies surrounding the *Bull Unigenitus* affected several ecclesiastical entities and religious congregations in France. Cardinal Noailles initially opposed the Bull. Brother Saturnino Gallego has argued that such controversies helped put the issue of changes to the *Rule* of the Brothers on the back burner.

For this reason, we humbly beseech you, and we command you in the name of the body of this Society to which you have vowed obedience, to resume forthwith the general conduct of its affairs.

In testimony of which, we have signed.

Done at Paris, 1 April 1714.

We are, with the most profound respect, dear father, your very humble and very obedient inferiors.

That letter was like the light at the end of the dark tunnel. It was a declaration of affection and recognition of the Founder and all he has done for our Society. In it, finally, could be read between the lines that we, the Brothers, spoke the same language as our dearest Father De La Salle. As the letter contained an explicit order, he obeyed and returned to Paris. Those who received him there say that when he arrived, he said: "Here I am; what do you want from me?" Words are lacking to describe that moment of joy.

From then on, all the details had to be adjusted to inaugurate a new era for the Institute. On the horizon appeared an opportunity for renewal, our presence in the city of Rouen. This helped to relieve many tensions in Paris.

Representation of "The Wall", property of the General Hospital of Rouen, where a Lasallian school operated.

On the other hand, it was necessary to begin the process of preparation for a General Chapter.

By then, I had already left Grenoble; and it was my turn to be the director of the Brothers in Paris.

The General Chapter opened on May 18, 1717. We elected the new Superior of our Society, Brother Barthélemy, who asked two Brothers to help him in the task of managing and animating. Brother Jean Le Roux, from Rheims, and I were elected to carry out this task. And while we have made every effort to make things right, there have been times when we have made mistakes, such as that contract we made with Monsieur Charon to send Brothers to Canada.[65] De La Salle intervened opportunely, as it was later shown that Charon, contrary to the Institute's direction, planned to separate the Brothers from the Society. As our father has said, "God guides things with wisdom and gentleness," and so that decision turned out to be providential.

Two years later, on Good Friday, April 7, 1719, our beloved father, De La Salle, died in Rouen. Before departing this world, he dedicated himself to writing down all that was necessary for the proper functioning of the communities of the *Brothers of the Christian Schools*. Of those writings, he himself was a living example. Certainly, Father De La Salle is a saint whose name is written in capital letters in the sky and in the heart of so many children and of every Brother.

---

[65] In Rouen, the sixteen Brothers of Saint Yon gave power to Brother Barthélemy and Brother Jean to sign a contract with Monsieur François Charon de La Barre to make a foundation in Canada. This was a second attempt, as there seemed to have been a precedent of negotiations with De La Salle in April 1700. On that occasion, the operation failed due to the shortage of personnel, but above all, the vocational incompatibility of the Brothers with the intended functions of caring for a hospital for orphans and severely incapacitated people. Probably, the same reasons and the strong reaction of the Founder as cited in the text prevented the signing of the contract, even though the tickets for the four Brothers had already been purchased.

The following year, Brother Barthélemy also passed away. We had to call another General Chapter to elect a new Superior. I presided over that chapter session, in which Brother Timothée was elected.

In those years and the years that followed, we began the task of tracking down remembrances about Father De La Salle.

We asked for testimonies, and we began the process of writing a biography that we entrusted to Brother Bernard. I remember writing to Brother Bernard asking him to revise that biography, which served as the basis for a second one written by his nephew Dom Élie-François Maillefer, a Benedictine religious of the Congregation of Saint Maur.

The year 1725 undoubtedly marked a moment of great happiness for our Society. Pope Benedict XIII approved the *Institute of the Brothers of the Christian Schools*, with the *Bull In apostolicae dignitatis solio.* On August 6th of that year, we convoked a General Chapter to receive the papal document, which was solemnly recognized nine days later.

On that occasion, we Chapter members, known as capitulants, made our vows according to the formula of vows that conformed to the Bull.

Pope Benedict XIII.

More than fifty years have passed since those young years in the school of my village of Chateau-Porcien, in which God lit in my heart the flame of the vocation to be a Brother. Today, that fire still continues to burn.

I now have the good fortune to be in Rouen and to be able to visit the tomb of our Father John-Baptist from time to time.

Apse of the Saint-Yon chapel. To the left was formerly the
Brothers' cemetery.

Closing my eyes, I can perceive his light that continues to shine brightly, inspiring new generations of Brothers fully consecrated to God in the Christian schools.

Jean Jacquot

Brother Jean Jacquot
Rouen, 1750

Texts Consulted for the Writing of This Chapter

- De La Salle, John-Baptist. *The Conduct of the Christian Schools.* Translated by F. de La Fontanerie and Richard Arnandez FSC and edited by William Mann FSC. Landover, MD: Lasallian Publications, 1996.

- De La Salle, John-Baptist. *The Duties of a Christian to God.* Translated by Richard Arnandez FSC and edited by Alexis James Doval. Landover, MD: Lasallian Publications, 2002.

- De La Salle, John-Baptist. "Rule of 1705 and Rule of 1718" in *Rule and Foundational Documents by John Baptist de La Salle.* Translated and edited by Augustine Loes FSC and Ronald Isetti. Landover, MD: Lasallian Publications, 2002. Pages 13-146.

- Gallego FSC, Saturnino. *The Life and Thought of John Baptist de La Salle* (vol. 1). Translated by Richard M. Orona FSC. Napa, CA: Lasallian Resource Center, tbd.

- Hours, Bernard. Jean-Baptiste de La Salle: *A Mystic in Action.* Translated by Anna Fitzgerald. Washington, DC: Christian Brothers Conference, 2022.

- Loes FSC, Augustine. *The First De La Salle Brothers: 1681-1719.* Landover, MD: Lasallian Publications, 1999.

- Valladolid FSC, José María. *Lasallian Chronology.* Lasalliana (no. 31). Rome: FSC, 1994.

- Valladolid FSC, José María. *Las cuatro primeras Biografías de San Juan Bautista de La Salle. Tomo IV. Índices de lugares, de personas, analítico y cronológico.* Madrid: La Salle Ediciones, 2010.

Memoirs of a Novice

Brother Stanislas (1698-1731)[66]

Funeral procession of Father John-Baptist de La Salle.

F|ather De La Salle has died," echoed in the corridors of the house of Saint Yon. "The saint is dead," resounded also in the episcopal palace of Rouen. In the early morning of Good Friday, 1719, our father and Founder departed for eternity. "I adore in all things the will of God in my regard," were his last words before Brother Barthélemy who kept watch all night at his deathbed. During the day, countless people came to the house to venerate him.

---

[66] Brother Stanislas (Albin Boucher) was, in September 1717, the second Brother to take this name in the Institute. The first died in August of the same year. Brother Stanislas is one of the Brothers who, according to biographer Canon Jean-Baptiste Blain, "died in the odor of sanctity." Blain places him on the path of perfection by his assiduous practice of prayer, humility, mortification, and all the other virtues of the Christian life. He was in Saint Yon in 1718, when the document for the purchase of the property was signed, as well as in Marseilles in 1727. That is when the Brothers petitioned the municipality for recognition as a religious congregation. Brother Stanislas was also in Avignon, in 1728, making vows in accordance with the new formula in accordance with the Institute's Bull of Approbation. In addition to being director of novices, he also served as Visitor for the communities of the South.

The next day, he was buried in the side chapel of Sainte-Suzanne in the parish of Saint-Sever, accompanied by a crowd gathered to bid him farewell. From that point on, we had an intercessor in heaven.[67]

That Holy Week had been different from previous ones. Our father was ill and close to death, but he remained lucid until the end.

Days before, on Monday of Holy Week, he had validated his will before a notary. That document read:

John-Baptist de La Salle convalescent.

In the name of the Father, and of the Son, and of the Holy Spirit. Amen. I, the undersigned John-Baptist de La Salle, priest, being sick in a room near the chapel of the house of Saint Yon, in the faubourg of Saint-Sever in the city of Rouen, wishing to make a testament to conclude all the matters that remain in my charge, I recommend to God first of all my own soul, and then all the Brothers of the Society of the Christian Schools with whom He has united me.

I urge them above all else always to have entire submission to the Church, especially in these evil times and, in order to give proof of this, never to separate themselves from the Church of Rome, always remembering that I sent two Brothers to Rome to ask God for the grace that their Society be always entirely submissive to it.

---

[67] After his death, devotion to John-Baptist de La Salle spread among the people and the Brothers. There were numerous testimonies of healings attributed to him.

I also recommend to them to have a great devotion to Our Lord. To have a great love for Holy Communion and the practice of meditation, to have a special devotion to the Most Blessed Virgin and to Saint Joseph, the patron and protector of their Society, and to fulfill their assignments with great zeal and without self-interest, to have a close union among themselves and blind obedience toward their superiors, which is the foundation and support of all perfection in a community.

The review of these lines takes me back to my youthful days, when Father De La Salle devoted much of his time to our formation.

He would say that it was one of his priorities, for he knew well that the future of the Institute depended largely on the novices being well-formed and very observant. Even more so in those times when the Church was going through difficult days.[68]

To remain united with the Church in Rome was one of the most recurrent exhortations in the community. Father De La Salle preached it with complete clarity and, moreover, wrote it down in the *Meditation for the Chair of Saint Peter.*

---

[68] During the Founder's lifetime, there was a strong dispute in the French Church over Jansenism, a religious movement emphasizing original sin, human perversion, and the need for divine grace for salvation. Grace predestined man from birth, and he could do nothing to change his fate. The controversy began with a book in Latin called *Augustinius* by Cornelius Jansen (1585-1638). It inspired Pasquier Quesnel (1634-1719) to publish *"Moral Reflections on the New Testament,"* which contained one hundred one propositions considered heretical. These were condemned by the *Bull Unigenitus Dei Filius* of Pope Clement XI. This Bull brought division among the French clergy. On February 5, 1714, forty bishops accepted the Bull at the Synod of Paris; and nine of them rejected it, among them Louis-Antoine de Noailles, Cardinal-Archbishop of Paris with whom the Founder had dealings on several occasions. During the year, one hundred twelve dioceses out of one hundred twenty-six would publish the Bull. De La Salle read the Bull during his stay in Grenoble. His stance in favor of acceptance and fidelity to the Church in Rome generated division among his family and some friends.

The Pope, being the Vicar of Jesus Christ and the visible head of the Church as well as the successor of Saint Peter, has wide authority over the entire Church, and all the faithful who are its members should look upon him as their father and as the voice God uses to give His orders to them.

He possesses the universal power of binding and loosing that Jesus Christ gave to Saint Peter; and to him Jesus Christ has committed the responsibility, first given to the holy apostle, of tending His flock.

Your role, then, is to work in order to increase and take care of the sheepfold; you should, therefore, honor our Holy Father, the Pope, as the holy shepherd of this flock and as the High Priest of the Church. You should respect his every word. It should be enough that something comes from him for you to be infinitely attentive [...] Adore God's authority in this sovereign Shepherd of souls, and in the future look upon him as the great teacher of the Church.[69]

The collection of the *Meditations* is just one of the many writings bequeathed to us by our father. I think we have learned more from his life than from his writings. While we lived with him in the novitiate of Saint Yon, we were able to witness that everything he wrote was validated by his example.

---

[69] It is Meditation #106.2. Moreover, in a letter to the Brother Director of Calais, dated January 28, 1719, De La Salle wrote: "I never thought of appealing, nor even of embracing the doctrine of the appellants to the future Council. I have too much respect for our Holy Father the Pope and too much submission to the decisions of the Holy See not to abide by them [...] It is enough for me that the person who sits today in the Chair of Saint Peter has declared by means of a Bull, accepted by almost all the bishops of the world, and that he has condemned the one hundred one propositions taken from the book of Father Quesnel, so that after such an authentic decision of the Church, I can say with Saint Augustine that the cause is finished. That is my feeling and my disposition, which was never different, and which I will never change." The Founder also wrote for the Brothers an instruction to guide them procedurally on this subject.

The devotion that he himself professed to Our Lord was instilled in us in many ways. We knew that to be Ministers of Christ we had to be progressively configured to Him. This required a demanding process of imitation, conformity, participation, and inner union with Our Lord. Christ is the model to follow and imitate in our ministry. Father De La Salle repeated this to us many times. We should imitate the humility of the Master who washed the feet of His disciples, or be like the Good Shepherd, who knows His sheep, each one, and feels great tenderness for them, to the point of giving His life for them.

This might sound like only a nice theological synthesis if Father De La Salle himself had not shown this by lived example. His room at Saint Yon was small and damp. In fact, it had served as a stable before he lived there. A very modest bed, a table, two chairs, and a crucifix were all there were in that space that he himself carefully swept until, because of his illness, he could no longer do so.

John-Baptist de La Salle, the writer, who systemized the organizational, educational and spiritual practices of the Brothers of the Christian Schools.

We were all greatly edified to see him take up the most humble and mortifying tasks.

And what about the imitation of the Good Shepherd? The community of Saint Yon, in its entirety,[70] can attest to this, especially the novices. He spent a lot of time sharing with us. Without a doubt, he was like the Good Shepherd who cared for each one of us with love and sensitivity.

---

[70] After the Parisian conflicts, the novitiate for the training of Brothers was set up in Saint Yon, which also housed a boarding school, a reformatory, and a detention center for those imprisoned by royal letters without first having gone through a trial. In many cases, these were persons of noble birth whose conduct was deemed dishonorable to society and their families.

He was always fervent in the recitation of the office, and the confessions were simply transformative for those of us who were blessed to celebrate that sacrament with him. But his care was not limited only to the novices; he also lavished time and effort on the boarding school students and the inmates, i.e., the inhabitants of the reformatory and the detention center housed at Saint Yon.

Our father, Father De La Salle, taught us that the imitation of Christ requires the Christian to conform progressively to the virtues of Our Lord; that is, to inwardly appropriate the Master's attitudes and express them in our behavior. He put great emphasis on the sufferings and humiliations that Our Lord experienced in His passion and death.

Two scenes in Father De La Salle's life have left a deep impression on me and exemplify what he preached. At Saint Yon, we had a horse, which I understand was given to Father De La Salle by Mademoiselle Lescure of Mende on account of a long journey he was to make from Mende to Avignon and Grenoble.

Well, one day, the steed went to graze in the orchard of a neighbor's farm. The owner, furious, slapped our father while he was praying the office. His reaction was to get down on his knees and ask for forgiveness.

The other episode was about a bad taste that certain Brothers experienced when they were going to Mass at Saint Nicoise, where some drunken soldiers attacked them. The Brothers denounced the soldiers, and the men were arrested. They were released after apologizing and doing so in writing. That the Brothers had denounced the soldiers displeased our father, because, in imitation of Christ, he felt that the Brothers should have been willing to accept suffering and be glad when they are found worthy to suffer reproaches in the name of Jesus.

Those events only reinforced the biblical truth so often repeated in the scriptures[71] that by sharing in Christ's sufferings and death, we enter His glory.

To imitate Christ, to conform to His attitudes, and to express them in our consecrated life requires a union as vital to Father De La Salle as that expressed in the lesson of the vine and the branches. Just as the branches are part of the vine, the Brothers are to participate in the mission of Jesus Christ by proclaiming the Gospel.

The Brothers are called to be a faithful reflection of Our Lord for children. This is what our father wrote to us:

> *It is Jesus Christ Himself who desires your disciples to look upon you as they would look upon Him, and to receive your instructions as if He in person were giving them to them, convinced that the truth of Jesus Christ speaks through your mouth.*

In a text Father De La Salle wrote for the novices, during his stay at the Seminary of Saint Nicolas du Chardonnet, the Explanation of the *Method of Interior Prayer,* [72] there were two parts in which we Brothers were encouraged to make acts of union with Our Lord.

EXPLICATION
DE LA MÉTODE
D'ORAISON.
Par Messire J. B. De La Salle, Instituteur des Frères des Écoles Chrétiennes.
PREMIÈRE PARTIE.

M. DCC XXXIX.

Title page of the *Explanation of the Method of Interior Prayer.*

---

[71] Some scriptural quotations: Hebrews 9:11-15, 10: 5-7; Colossian 2:11, 13-14; Galatians 5:24.

[72] The "*Method of Interior Prayer*" had already been published in the Collection of Various Short Treatises around 1711. The text in question explains each part and act around a mystery, a virtue, or an evangelical maxim on which the prayer is centered. As far as the presence of God is concerned, there is an important development both in the work as a whole and in the corpus of Lasallian writings.

I remember with great affection how Father De La Salle paid special attention to teaching us this "*Method*" each day before lunch. In another of his meditations, Father De La Salle wrote,

> *Unite all your actions to those of Jesus Christ Our Lord, so that, sanctified by your merits and anointing, you may be pleasing to God and a means of salvation for others.*

Undoubtedly, the whole life of the Brother is to be integrated from this perspective so that he can say with Saint Paul: "It is no longer I who live, but Christ who lives in me" (Gal 2:20).

To remain united to Our Lord, our father exhorted us to deeply love Holy Communion. Some of those phrases that were written in his meditations still reverberate in my memory:

> *See to it that Holy Communion may produce between Jesus Christ and you such a constant union that you will never be separated from Him.*

> *How happy they must be to live in a state in which, communion being so frequent, they can always be one and form only one with Jesus Christ, possess His Spirit, and work only through Him!*

This teaching could be said in many ways, but the best thing was his example. On Wednesday of Holy Week, already very weakened by the ailments of the illness that afflicted him, he devoted the whole day to preparing to receive Holy Communion. He awaited the coming of Our Lord in the Eucharist as he was seated; but as soon as the bell rang to announce His approach, our father fell on his knees to receive Him. How can we wipe from our eyes the emotion we felt at witnessing that demonstration of sublime love?

The deep love professed by our father for Our Lord, consequently, led us as Brothers to love His Mother, the Virgin Mary.

This is how Father De La Salle explained it to us in his Meditation for the Day of the Octave of the Immaculate Conception.

> *The holy religious state, to which God has had the goodness to call us, is our mother; the novitiate is her womb in which she spiritually conceives the novices who are her children; she enlightens them for Jesus Christ, as Saint Paul expresses it, by forming them to a truly Christian and religious way in life.*[73]

Devotion to Saint Joseph, patron and protector of our Society, was so closely linked to our ministry that Father De La Salle gave him to us as an example to imitate in the virtuous care he lavished on the Child Jesus.

> *You must have a similar attention and affection for preserving or procuring the innocence of the children entrusted to your guidance, and to keep them away from whatever might interfere with their education or prevent them from acquiring piety, just as Saint Joseph had for all that could contribute to the welfare of the Child Jesus. For you have been made responsible for these children just as Saint Joseph was made responsible by God for the Savior of the world.*[74]

Diligence and affection, a love that selflessly cares for poor children, has been for me a synthesis of those years, in which I also witnessed how our father took care to accompany the Brothers in their particular needs. For him, this meant putting all his gifts at the service of organizing, leading, and animating a Community that was often in danger of perishing.

He also put his gifts as a writer at the service of systematizing everything that the Society needed for its subsistence and spiritual-ministerial unity.

---

[73] Meditation #83.2.
[74] Meditation #110.3.

To this end, he devoted his last years at Saint Yon. He composed texts[75] and corrected others that were already in force for the Society. Both in his writings and in his life, he gave himself entirely as the spiritual father of the Brothers of the Christian Schools.

How can we forget his benevolence toward all, his smiling face, and his always charitable and humble gestures? Such was his humility that, at times, it even created discomfort for a clergy who could not allow for the idea of a priest submitting to the authority of a layman (a Brother). However, he himself set an example of the obedience that he urged us to embrace. On one occasion, Brother Barthélemy revealed part of what Father De La Salle wrote to him in a letter:

> *I am in a position to attend the main events of the community like the others, and to sleep in the common dormitory, and to eat the food everyone else eats in the refectory; I beg you not to oppose it.*

The time spent in the novitiate of Saint Yon has been etched in my life. As I look back on all that I have learned, a deep joy fills my soul for all that God has allowed me to witness.

Some time has passed since those years; but like our mother Mary, I have kept all these things in my heart that I might be able to share them with the new generations of Brothers that I have to form today, being the director of the novitiate of Avignon.

Brother Stanislas

---

[75] It is probable that the *"Meditations for the Time of Retreat"* was composed at this time of his life and that he, also at this time, corrected the *"Meditations for Sundays and the Principal Feasts"* as well. Undoubtedly, the *Rule* of 1718 was also written at Saint Yon.

Texts Consulted for the Writing of This Chapter

- De La Salle, John-Baptist. *Collection of Various Short Treatises.* Translated by William J. Battersby FSC and edited by Daniel Burke FSC. Landover, MD: Lasallian Publications, 1993.

- De La Salle, John-Baptist. *Explanation of the Method of Interior Prayer.* Translated by Richard Arnandez FSC and edited by Donald Mouton FSC. Landover, MD: Lasallian Publications, 1995.

- De La Salle, John-Baptist. *Meditations.* Translated by Richard Arnandez FSC and Augustine Loes FSC and edited by Augustine Loes FSC and Francis Huether FSC. Landover, MD: Lasallian Publications, 1994.

- Gallego FSC, Saturnino. *The Life and Thought of John Baptist de La Salle* (vol. 1). Translated by Richard M. Orona FSC. Napa, CA: Lasallian Resource Center, tbd.

- Hours, Bernard. *Jean-Baptiste de La Salle: A Mystic in Action.* Translated by Anna Fitzgerald. Washington, DC: Christian Brothers Conference, 2022.

- Loes FSC, Augustine. *The First De La Salle Brothers: 1681-1719.* Landover, MD: Lasallian Publications, 1999.

- Valladolid FSC, José María. *Lasallian Chronology.* Lasalliana (no. 31). Rome: FSC, 1994.

- Valladolid FSC, José María. *Las cuatro primeras Biografías de San Juan Bautista de La Salle. Tomo IV. Índices de lugares, de personas, analítico y cronológico.* Madrid: La Salle Ediciones, 2010.

Meeting De La Salle Today

Brother Hernán Santos (1976 -)

When my family and I moved from the countryside to the house of Fernando de la Mora, everything was new to me: the paved road, the traffic lights, the school, the electric lights during the day, the cartoons, the neighborhood, and friends. I remember one Saturday morning, my mother told me that I should continue with First Communion catechesis. When I asked her where, she said, "At La Salle." I kept wondering what it was. That afternoon, I got the surprise of my life. I found a place and a time set aside for the children. There were many of us. Several of my friends from the neighborhood and some classmates from school were also there.

That day, I also learned what a Brother was. A guy for whom the children had a very special affection. None of us wanted to miss the opportunity to share with Brother Roberto Echegaray, even if it was only a greeting. There, the recesses were much longer than those at my prior school; and there was so much space to play, run, and have fun. In a very short time, for me, going to La Salle was the most awaited moment of the week. There was Roberto, always joyful, along with other aspirants and catechists. That space had everything: children's songs with accordion, puppets, kites being remounted, children's festivities of San Juan [San Juan Ara], and religious celebrations of Christmas and Easter.

There, we sang together in the chapel; and the "Forever" that came after the salutation "Live Jesus in our hearts" deafened more than one of us for a few seconds and made the windowpanes vibrate.

After Confirmation, I joined the team of catechists. At that point in my life, I began to question my faith and commitment as a young Christian. At the entrance to the community house, on one of the windows, there was a sticker that read "La Salle, sign of faith." Whenever I saw it, I wondered what that meant. Little by little, I got to know more Brothers. I was very struck by their serenity and people skills.

It didn't take long for me, along with other friends, to frequent the community. It was on one of those afternoons of shared *"tereré"*[76] that we were invited to get to know the work in a school located in the suburbs of Asuncion. When we arrived and started walking around Fatima's neighborhood, meeting local people and the school project, I could understand that "La Salle" was also a sign of faith and hope for children immersed in poverty. A condition of which, I must confess, I was profoundly unaware. Thousands of questions arose in my heart by storm with that visit. To these questions were added those that came after knowing other schools in Pozo, Colorado, and Cerrito.

"La Salle" was that word that echoed in my head as I was arranging the letters in the typesetting of the printing house where I worked.

"La Salle and those poor children and young people" were words that occupied my thoughts when I sat down at night to look at the stars from the balcony of my house.

I don't really know the moment, nor the circumstances in which I decided to leave my job as a

Children eating grapes and melon, by Bartolomé Esteban Murillo.

---

[76] A Paraguayan cold-brewed infusion of yerba mate, herbs, and water similar to the "mate" earlier referenced.

typographer to respond to that strong call of Jesus to join the Lasallian project.

In my stages of formation to become a Brother, I discovered that "La Salle" also inspired many educational, pastoral, spiritual, catechetical, and social experiences in many other countries. Particularly, in all those years of formation, "La Salle" meant for me vital redemption and adherence to the person of Jesus and His project.

I embraced the vocation of Brother on December 8, 2001. Since then, "La Salle" has had many meanings in my life. Undoubtedly, the experience of having lived for ten years in Malvinas Argentinas, the suburbs of Córdoba city, Argentina, has meant for me an existential place of discovery of other ways of thinking about education, together with talented educators who assumed the responsibility of transforming a challenging and complex reality as well as living my faith together with that beautiful neighborhood community.

For me, that small town became a theological-existential place to give the definitive "yes" of my consecration as a De La Salle Brother. In those days, the words associated with "La Salle" were communities of faith, formation of catechists, school, children, educational service to the poor…

The ways of God, who guides all things with wisdom and gentleness (sometimes!), as Brother Martin Digilio would say, brought me back five years ago to a corner of San Pedro,[77] where the experience of "La Salle" began, once again, to lay hold of renewed meanings.

The challenge of training teachers, both those who are beginning to dream of embracing this vocation and those who are already in the classroom, opened a door that, until then, had not been explored much by me in the Founder's life: his condition as

---

[77] San Pedro is a Department (like a State) in Paraguay. The Catholic Diocese has the same name.

formator of formators, a ministry to which De La Salle devoted much of his life.

The life-sustaining situation I inhabit today invites me to discover the figure of Saint John-Baptist de La Salle as an exceptional formator of novice teachers and a pedagogical-spiritual leader of a nascent and expanding community. Allow me to delve a little deeper into this line of reflection.

In the initial experience of the Community of Christian schools, the Founder noticed the lack of spiritual and didactic formation of those first teachers of the schools of Rheims who had been recruited by Adrian Nyel. Then, from that situation, De La Salle decided to receive them into his own home to better form them in matters related to spirituality and didactics. It can be said that this act marked the beginning of a mystical-active experience for the Founder, an experience that, with the passage of time and a process of permanent systematization of good practices in the schools, became the ministry of John-Baptist de La Salle.

In the years following that act, the Founder dedicated himself to organizing the formation of the Brothers for the mission by combining two aspects of a single reality inherent in the Christian school: spirituality and didactics, or we could say, a spirituality embodied in didactics. Both aspects required (even today) strenuous work in which several actors had to be involved. Now, where and how was this to be learned?

This learning was a result of the Lasallian community's own reflection on the insufficient initiation to integrating the teaching experience, community, and spiritual life. It was necessary, they discovered, to organize a novitiate where this formation would occur.

The novitiate lasted two years during the Founder's time. The first of these two years had a strong emphasis on spirituality.

That is, the novices learned to pray through a series of religious-spiritual exercises: interior prayer,[78] the recitation of community prayers, spiritual reading, and an asceticism still worthy of admiration. The Founder was particularly dedicated to forming the future Brothers in this dimension.

In the second year of the novitiate, the novices were sent to communities associated with the schools where they took their first steps as teachers, always accompanied by a Brother with proven expertise in the classroom. And, as it could not be otherwise, starting out as a novice teacher also required mediated and systematic accompaniment.

To this end, the novice Brother had to be deeply immersed in the Guide, or Conduct of the Christian Schools, which would be like a manual of didactic practices. Another companion for the practices of the novice teacher was a *"Rule of the Formator of Novice [Beginning] Teachers."*[79]

Everything was designed and planned so that the new teacher would integrate into his life, which was consecrated to the education of the poor, a strong spirituality centered on the person of Jesus Christ, and a didactic that involved personal work to configure his character according to what the school mission required. That is, for the teacher to educate by example, being for the poor children who attend the Christian schools, a minister of Jesus Christ present in their midst.[80] This is a dual dynamic.

---

[78] De La Salle composed a method for the interior prayer of the Brothers. Later, he wrote the *Explanation of the Method of Interior Prayer* with a view to the formation of the novices.

[79] Cf. "Appendix C: The Training of New Teachers" in *The Conduct of the Christian Schools* by John-Baptist de La Salle, translated by F. de La Fontanerie and Richard Arnandez FSC, and edited by William Mann FSC (Landover, MD: Lasallian Publications, 1996), pages 255-270.

[80] The *"Meditations for the Time of Retreat,"* the Founder's exceptional work, states this most specifically in Meditation #201.

The Brother, also, had to discover Christ in the poor children he was educating.[81]

That foundational experience of John-Baptist de La Salle and the first communities of Brothers constitutes, for those of us who identify as Lasallians today, a "subversive memory" in the task we have of forming new generations of teachers within an educational and religious community.

It is a living memory, permanently inviting the re-invention of practices, spirituality, schools, and feelings.

The biographical narratives in various voices we have presented in this small book seek to discover the human situations that those men and women experienced and the profound experience of God's passage through their situations. This step is often imperceptible and can only be seen with the eyes of faith.

It is the same challenge we face today as we go about our daily lives in the communities and educational institutions to which we belong. The invitation remains for those who want to continue delving into the madness of following Jesus in the ministry of the Christian educator.

Live Jesus in our hearts! Forever!

Brother Hernán

---

[81] This can be noted, for example, in the *Meditations* #173.1, #80.3, and #96.3 among others.

Made in the USA
Middletown, DE
14 November 2024

64591104R00069